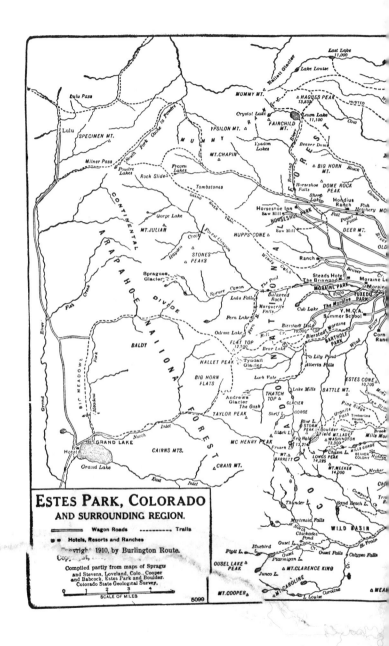

MOUNTAINEERING IN COLORADO.

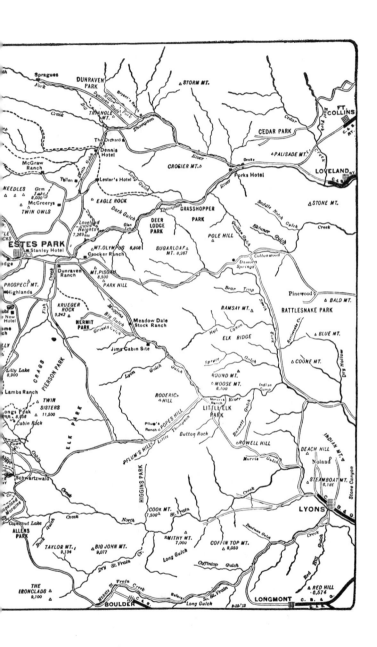

LONG'S PEAK FROM TABLE MOUNTAIN.

Mountaineering in Colorado

THE PEAKS ABOUT ESTES PARK

by

FREDERICK H. CHAPIN

Foreword and Notes by James H. Pickering

University of Nebraska Press
Lincoln and London

First Bison Book printing: 1987
Most recent printing indicated by the first digit below:
1   2   3   4   5   6   7   8   9   10

Library of Congress Cataloging-in-Publication Data
Chapin, Frederick H. (Frederick Hastings)
    Mountaineering in Colorado.
    Reprint. Originally published: Boston:
Appalachian Mountain Club, 1889.
    Bibliography: p.
    1. Mountaineering — Colorado — Estes Park Region —
Guide-books. 2. Estes Park Region (Colo.) —
Description and travel — Guide-books. I. Title.
GV199.42.C62E833 1987   917.88'69   86-25105
ISBN 0-8032-1437-5
ISBN 0-8032-6322-8 (pbk.)

This Bison Book reproduces the 1889 edition published by the Appalachian Mountain Club, Boston, Massachusetts. To this edition a foreword with two photographs, notes for the entire volume, and a map have been added.

The map on pp. ii–iii is an early promotional map of Estes Park by the Burlington Railroad Company, based on the Cooper-Babcock Map of 1903. Some small errors were made in the original transcription.

FOREWORD
by James H. Pickering

Frederick Hastings Chapin's *Mountaineering in Colorado: The Peaks about Estes Park,* published at Boston in 1889 under the auspices of the Appalachian Mountain Club, has long been recognized as a classic of Colorado's mountaineering literature. As the modern reader will discover, much of the charm of Chapin's book lies simply in its subject matter. Mountains, particularly picturesque mountains, exert a timeless fascination. They are there, old but ever new, to be recognized, viewed, climbed, and otherwise enjoyed by generation after generation. That the mountains Frederick Chapin writes about happen to be the spectacular peaks clustered together along Colorado's northern Front Range makes *Mountaineering in Colorado* of particular interest to the many thousands of visitors from all over the world who have developed a special and long-standing relationship with the scenic beauty and rugged backcountry of Estes Park, Colorado.

Chapin's small book is also of interest and importance because it belongs, historically, to an Estes Park that in some ways is quite different from the one most of us know. The years 1887 and 1888 were for Estes Park clearly ones of transition. Some thirty years had passed since that day in mid-October of 1859 when Joel Estes and his son, following the Little Thompson westward into the mountains on a hunting and exploring expedition, gazed down from the top of Park Hill upon the spectacular valley (or "park" in the parlance of the mountains) that would soon bear his name. In that interval, the first settlers had arrived. Families like the Spragues, Fergusons, MacGregors, Lambs, and Jameses had taken up their 160-acre homesteads and built, and in most cases already improved, their first sod-roofed log cabins. They had also discovered, however begrudgingly in some cases, that the economic future of their lovely, sequestered mountain valley rested in no small measure on its ability to cater to an ever-increasing number of summer visitors.

Of particular—and, as it would turn out, of lasting—importance to the Estes Park that Chapin and other early visitors would come to know was the role played by Windham Thomas Wyndam-Quin (1841–1926), the fourth Earl of Dunraven. Dunraven, a wealthy Irish lord, came to the park on a hunting expedition in late December 1872 and again in 1873 and 1874. Immediately enamored both with the scenery and the abundance of elk, deer, mountain sheep, and other game, the earl soon launched an ambitious attempt to gain control of the park for a private hunting preserve. Dunraven consulted lawyers in Denver, who told him that in order to control and fence the park he must gain legal title to all lands on which there were springs or streams. To carry out this grand design Dunraven employed as his agent one Theodore Whyte, an Irish mining engineer, who set about orchestrating the filing of claims (many of them, as it turned out, fraudulent) under the Homestead Act of 1862. When the hunting preserve idea had to be abandoned because of the violent opposition of already established residents and an aroused Colorado press, Dunraven organized the Estes Park Company, Ltd. (or English Company, as it came to be known). This joint-stock undertaking turned the land already acquired—upwards of 15,000 acres—over to the care and feeding of both cattle and vacationists. Though the company never made money at either, the earl's ownership, which lasted until 1907, kept together in one piece large tracts of land, thus retarding the kind of unbridled development that would overtake Estes Park in the years that followed. "We all began to see," pioneer Abner Sprague noted some years later, "that the holding of so much of the Park by one company, even if it had been secured unlawfully, was the best thing for the place, particularly after it was proven that the place was only valuable because of its location, and its attraction for the lovers of the out-of-doors."[1]

By the time that Frederick Chapin, his wife Alice, and their friends arrived for the summers of 1887 and 1888, the beginning of that tourist industry was well underway. Thanks to a growing body of guidebooks, histories, travel narratives, gazetteers, city directories, and magazine "sketches"—much of it frankly promotional—Colorado was becoming increasingly well known as a safe, scenic, healthful and accessible place for summer vacations. Estes Park, too, shared in this boosterism. "Tourists seeking new scenes in nature," boasted the *Denver Republican* in 1881, "could not do better than to visit this famous nook of the Rockies and epicures hunting a mountain retreat where they can live with all the table delicacies and luxuries of a metropolis can find such an institution in Estes Park."[2] To the efforts of the print media was added the widening circulation of the striking black and white photographs by William Henry Jackson. Taken in 1873, 1874, and 1875, while Jackson was head of the Hayden Survey's photographic division, these pictures established the spectacular beauty of Colorado and other parts of the Rocky Mountain West firmly in the American mind.[3] Visitors to Estes Park in 1887 had their choice of accommodations. They could stay at Dunraven's large—and comparatively expensive—English Hotel on lower Fish Creek Road or at one of the small number of so-called ranches that dotted the valley. Or they could, as many preferred, simply pitch a tent for the season along the banks of one of the many streams in the park. They came to fish, to hunt, or simply to recreate. Many, like Alice Chapin, came for reasons of health, for the dry, rarefied air of the Rocky Mountains, which was widely prescribed by climatologists as the best antidote and cure for those with pulmonary ailments.

The magnet of the region, then as now, was majestic 14,255-foot Longs Peak, first climbed by Major John Wesley Powell, William Byers, editor of the *Rocky Mountain News,* and five others coming from Grand Lake by way of Wild Basin in 1868. By 1887, Carlyle Lamb and his father, the Reverend Elkanah Lamb, using the ranch they named Longs Peak House as their base of operations, had been taking parties up to the summit of the peak for some years. Their fee was five dollars, making the Lambs among the first professional mountain guides in the state. But north of Longs Peak, in the wilderness area that would in 1915 become part of Rocky Mountain National Park, were mountains that were seldom, if ever, climbed. It was to these peaks that Frederick Chapin and his friends turned their attention. The stories of their climbs—a number of which turned out to be historic firsts and genuine explorations of discovery—comprise the narrative of Chapin's book.

Interestingly enough, for all his public activity, which included the publication of two books and a number of articles, relatively little is known about Frederick Chapin. What can be learned has been pieced together from a number of widely scattered sources—in Hartford, Connecticut; Lafayette, Indiana; Leavenworth, Kansas; Estes Park, Colorado; and elsewhere—with the help of the individuals whose contributions are acknowledged below.

Frederick Hastings Chapin was born in Lafayette, Indiana, on September 5, 1852, the son of Luther Van Horn Chapin (1819–?), a native of Hamilton, New York, and his wife, Angelina Delvira Hastings Chapin (1823–62), a native of Suffield, Connecticut.[4] Luther and Angelina were married on July 8, 1849, and by the following year Luther had established himself as a merchant in Lafayette, Indiana, on the banks of the Wabash River, perhaps in partnership with his widower father Asa Chapin (1787–1870).[5] Thanks to the completion of the Wabash and Erie Canal across the state, Lafayette had become by 1850 a busy, thriving town of some 6,000. That city "does more business in proportion to its population," remarked a visitor in 1853, "than any place with which we are acquainted. The amount of the produce shipped and of the goods sold there, is immense."[6]

Despite the business opportunities in Lafayette, the Chapins did not stay. Shortly after the birth of a daughter, Gertrude Eliza, in September 1856,[7] Luther and Angelina Chapin moved west to Leavenworth, Kansas, a town very much in its infancy. Founded in 1854 by pro-slavery men from Missouri who surged across the border into the Kansas Territory to claim the rich lands along the Missouri River, Leavenworth was a turbulent, and often brutal, frontier community. Though political sentiment slowly shifted in favor of the free soilers, the town's early years were filled with numerous acts of violence, including murders and public hangings, many of them politically inspired. Nevertheless, Leavenworth prospered and grew. The influx of new citizens was staggering. From 270 residents in 1855, the number grew to 2,800 by 1857, to 7,800 by 1860, and to 31,210 by 1867. "I am fully convinced," enthused a recent arrival in August 1857, that "it is the place to make money—no man can help making money here providing he is willing to 'rough' it. . . . Any business will pay here except doing nothing."[8]

The close proximity to Fort Leavenworth and its permanent garrison made the town the eastern terminus for both the Oregon and Santa Fe Trails. This advantage inevitably gave rise to huge commercial enterprises like the famous transportation firm of Russell, Majors, and Waddell, which dominated the shipping of freight across the plains. Fort Leavenworth was the general military depot that supplied the U.S. government's western outposts. In 1858–59 alone, the government contracted for sixteen million pounds of freight to be hauled over the Oregon Trail by Russell, Majors, and Waddell in caravans consisting of twenty-six wagons, each drawn by six yoke of oxen.

Once again Luther Chapin found employment as a salesman. The fact that he regularly changed jobs, and without apparent advancement,[9] suggests that life for the Chapins was neither settled nor easy. In March 1862, Angelina Chapin died, perhaps in childbirth, and Luther was suddenly left to raise ten-year-old Frederick and six-year-old Gertrude. Though Luther married again in July 1864,[10] he nevertheless decided to send both children back east to the home of their aunt, Mrs. Thomas Sisson, in Hartford, Connecticut. It was a decision that changed completely the course of Frederick Chapin's life.

However difficult life in Leavenworth might have been for adults, it was a decidedly exciting place for a young boy—particularly for a boy with imagination and an adventurous spirit. Such was apparently the case with Frederick Chapin, for an anonymous writer noted years later in the *Hartford Courant* that

> The boy spent much of his time around the barracks and was much interested in soldiers and army equipments. He loved the prairies and watched the Indians on the neighboring reservations with much interest. When, at the age of 10 years, he learned to ride horseback, he would frequently accompany the caravans for many miles out on the prairies. It was thus that Mr. Chapin acquired a love of adventure, travel and discovery, which influenced all the rest of his life.[11]

Hartford, Connecticut, was the antithesis of Leavenworth: cosmopolitan, conservative, well established, and a trifle complacent in its affluence. Visitors from other parts were not infrequently struck by the settled beauty of the place. One such visitor was none other than Samuel L. Clemens, whose own boyhood had been spent in the Mississippi River town of Hannibal, Missouri. At about the time the Chapin children arrived, Clemens was contemplating a move to Hartford. Writing in January 1868, he could scarcely contain his enthusiasm for the city he would call home from 1871 to 1891:

> I think this is the best built and the handsomest town I have ever seen. . . . They have the broadest, straightest streets in Hartford, that ever led a sinner to destruction, and the dwelling houses are the amplest in size, and the shapliest, and have the most capacious ornamental grounds about them. This is the centre of Connecticut wealth. Hartford dollars have a place in half the great moneyed enterprises of the union. All those Phoenix and Charter Oak Insurance Companies, whose gorgeous chromo-lithographic show cards it has been my delight to study in far-away cities, are located here.[12]

What particularly struck Mark Twain, as it surely must have struck Frederick Chapin, was the character of the landscape: "Everywhere the eye turns," he wrote in August 1868, "it is blessed with a vision of refreshing green. You do not know what beauty is if you have not been here."[13]

Thomas Sisson (1828–1907), his wife, the former Gertrude M. Hastings (1832–1910), and their two daughters lived at 126 Farmington Avenue in the affluent West Hartford that Mark Twain so admired.[14] As the head of Sisson and Butler, the oldest continuous wholesale and retail drug firm in Connecticut, Thomas Sisson was a part of the Hartford business establishment and one of the city's

Frederick Chapin as a young man, ca. 1877. Courtesy of Patricia Potter
Duncan.

leading citizens.[15] The Sissons raised Frederick Chapin
very much as they would have raised their own son. After a
year at the local district school and one year of high school,
Chapin, not yet fifteen, entered his uncle's drug business.
There is no evidence that Chapin ever returned to school,
much less attended college. What further education he received, he obtained largely on his own. Nevertheless,
Frederick Chapin became a well educated man. Not only
did he read widely, particularly in the literature of travel
and exploration,[16] but he developed an ability to write that
would have done credit to any collegian. Of equal importance, Chapin developed the poise and self-confidence that
allowed him to move easily in circles that included some of
the best trained and most intelligent men of his generation.

Chapin evidently discharged the responsibilities of his
apprenticeship well, for in 1881, at the age of twenty-nine,
he was admitted to partnership in Sisson, Chandler, and
Chapin (as the firm was renamed). With this advancement
came the money and the leisure to travel and to pursue
avocational interests. In the case of Frederick Chapin, as
in the case of a growing number of his professional and
middle-class contemporaries, these interests included an
enthusiasm for mountains and mountaineering. What began with "Mounts Tom and Holyoke, and Connecticut
hills,"[17] and visits to the Adirondacks[18] and White Mountains, would lead Chapin over a period of some seventeen
years to the Swiss Alps, to the mountains of Colorado, and
to the Himalayas of northern India.

Chapin first visited Switzerland in the summer of 1877,
just prior to his twenty-fifth birthday, in the company of
three other New Englanders. One of them was Charles P.
Howard of Hartford, a life-long friend and fellow mountain
enthusiast, who would later accompany Chapin to Colorado.[19] Though the young Americans dutifully spent
time in both England and France, their real objective was

the mountains of Switzerland. With Baedeker's *Switzerland* in hand, they moved quickly across the terrain:

> We first crossed the Spulgen Pass from Lake Zurich to Lake Como, and then crossed the Alps again, going from Lake Maggiore to Lake Lucerne by way of the St. Gotthard. After ascending the Rigi, we spent a few days in the Bernese Oberland and on Lake Thun, and then, from the summit of the Gemmi Pass, we had our first view of the grandest region in this mountainous country, — that is, the Monte Rosa chain and its neighboring peaks. Down the winding stairway-like road of the Gemmi, we ran a neck-and-neck race for the baths of Leuk, and thence to Visp.[20]

Beyond Visp lay Zermatt and the towering Matterhorn, the "last great problem of the Alps," first climbed just twelve years before in June 1865 by Edward Whymper at the cost of four members of his party. Charles Howard was apparently a more experienced mountaineer than the others, for he elected to take on the Matterhorn, a feat he described in the September 1879 issue of *Lippincott's Magazine*.[21] Chapin and the others settled for the 13,685-foot Breithorn, which they "accomplished . . . without much fatigue, and with little thought of rarefied air."[22]

From Zermatt they walked and rode to the village of Chamonix in order to climb 15,782-foot Mont Blanc, still regarded as a considerable accomplishment. Joined by another American, Chapin and his party, with the aid of four guides, two porters, and a mule, left Chamonix on the morning of August 8th for what was to be an unforgettable experience. ("Why we took the mule," Chapin would later confess, "I do not remember, but it was probably for the benefit of the guides."[23]) That afternoon they ran into bad weather and were forced to take refuge in a low and narrow hut, where they spent the night, alternately fighting fleas and listening to the thunder of nearby avalanches. After a false start, a retreat, and a second dismal night in the mountain hut, Chapin and his party reached the summit of Mont Blanc before eight o'clock on the morning of August 10th. It was a hard-won moment to be savored:

> We stood in line on [the narrow ridge of the summit] . . . and turned to view the landscape. Many writers among climbing fraternities disparage the view from Mont Blanc, but I never have had such a sight, before or since, and I never expect to have such a view again. . . . All the Zermatt group—Monte Rosa, the Matterhorn, the Weisshorn, and the Breithorn, which we knew so well—and the range of the Grand Combin, seemed right upon us; the whole making an impression upon our minds not to be obliterated till memory is no more.[24]

On May 25, 1882, Frederick Chapin married Alice Louise Seavey of West Hartford[25] and promptly set out on a honeymoon trip that included a return visit to the Swiss Alps. The objective on this occasion was the 13,855-foot Zinal Rothhorn, rising some 8,540 feet above the village of Zermatt, and offering a "fine survey of the Vispthal" below. Accompanied by two guides and a porter, Chapin set out on the five-hour climb to the summit on the afternoon of June 24, 1882. After passing an uneventful night on the mountain, the climb resumed and they reached their destination, without incident, by 8:30 A.M. the following morning.

Having made first-hand acquaintance with the great mountains of Europe, Chapin next turned his attention to the Rocky Mountains of Colorado. Although it has been suggested that he made as many as eight separate visits to Colorado, only four trips—during the summers of 1886, 1887, 1888, and 1889—can be established with certainty. A major stimulus to Frederick Chapin's interest in mountains and mountaineering—as well as to his decision to write accounts of his experiences—was his growing participation in the activities of the Appalachian Mountain Club and his friendship with a number of its leading members. Founded at Boston's Institute of Technology in January 1876, the AMC established as its objectives "to explore the mountains of New England and the adjacent regions, both for scientific and artistic purposes; and, in general, to cultivate an interest in geographical studies."[26] By the time that Chapin's application for membership was approved, in late 1880 or early 1881,[27] the AMC had launched a quarterly journal, *Appalachia,* and had established an agenda of activities that included frequent mountain excursions and regular evening meetings at which members gathered to listen to papers, exchange information, and share fellowship.

Chapin's direct involvement with the AMC began in May 1885 when the account of his 1882 ascent of the Zinal Rothhorn was read to the membership by Professor Charles Fay. In the eight years that followed, Chapin submitted eight more written accounts of his expeditions, seven of which were subsequently published in *Appalachia.* For the five-year period between 1885 and 1890 Frederick Chapin proved to be the Appalachian Mountain Club's single most prolific contributor. His fields of interest ranged decidedly beyond New England. He became the first member to write about the Alps, and the first to submit a series of detailed accounts about the mountains of Colorado. His 1890 description of the recent new discoveries in the Mancos Canyon of the Mesa Verde extended the focus of the club to the field of Indian anthropology. By every indication Chapin's efforts were well received, and he developed pleasant and long-lasting friendships with several of his fellow Appalachians, most notably with Charles E. Fay, a professor of modern languages at Tufts College who served four terms as AMC president, and J.

Rayner Edmands, an assistant at the Harvard Observatory who over the years filled a variety of AMC offices, including councillor of topography and president.

We know little about Chapin's 1886 trip to Colorado other than the fact that he climbed Pikes Peak near Colorado Springs[28] and made a first visit to Estes Park. Though Chapin speaks in the Preface to *Mountaineering in Colorado* of "climbing some of the peaks [about Estes Park] in the autumn of 1886," these early explorations were apparently confined to the lower elevations. We do know, however, that Chapin brought his camera with him, and presumably used the occasion to practice the art of mountain photography, an interest that became an important part of Chapin's mountaineering.[29] These photographic efforts were aided greatly by the recent introduction of commercially available dry plates that both simplified the photographic process and reduced the amount of required equipment. By contrast, the photographic gear that William H. Jackson and other early American mountain photographers were forced to carry, including a darkroom tent, weighed upward of a hundred pounds. Though mountain photography by 1880 had been brought within the scope of the talented amateur, Chapin still had to contend with fragile glass plates and a fairly heavy camera and tripod — a burden that should add considerably to our appreciation of his results.[30]

Though local tradition has it that Chapin spent his first visit at W. E. James's Elkhorn ranch (the forerunner of the Elkhorn Lodge)[31] when he returned with Alice Chapin in July 1887, he stayed at Horace Ferguson's ranch resort, the Highlands, located just north of Marys Lake. Among the more interesting discoveries of that summer was the realization that most early visitors to Estes Park did not climb its rugged and inviting mountain peaks. Longs Peak, to be sure, attracted the attention of climbers, but probably no more than twenty parties attempted the sum-

mit in the course of a single season. To the north and west
of Longs Peak lay a virtually unknown wilderness. Even
as celebrated a mountaineer as Carlyle Lamb (1862–
1958), who conducted Chapin to the top of Longs Peak in
July 1887, and who had been guiding professionally since
1880, confessed that "he had never climbed any of the
elevations west of Longs Peak."[32] The absence of know-
ledgeable and willing guides posed a serious problem to
would-be mountaineers like Frederick Chapin. Fortunately, he made the acquaintance that summer of William Hallett (1851–1941), who, next to Abner Sprague, probably
had more first-hand knowledge about the mountains
around Estes Park than any other living individual. It was
Hallett who took Chapin up Flattop Mountain to visit Tyndall Glacier and the peak that Chapin would name for Hallett himself, and who then conducted Chapin and George
W. Thacher of Boston to the newly discovered Hallett (now
Rowe) Glacier to the north of Hagues Peak.

Returning to Hartford, Chapin used the succeeding fall
and winter months to publicize the attractions of Estes
Park. He wrote up his visit to Hallett Glacier for presentation to the Appalachian Mountain Club on the evening of
October 12, 1887, and then provided the photographs to
accompany its publication in the December 1887 issue of
Appalachia. He and Thacher also shared their enthusiasm
directly by issuing invitations to several of their fellow
Appalachians. As a result, plans were made and the following July Alice and Frederick Chapin, Mr. and Mrs.
George Thacher (Mrs. Thacher and Mrs. Chapin shared a
love for mountain flowers), Professor Charles Fay, and J.
Raynor Edmands all rendezvoused together at the Ferguson ranch.[33] Fay recalled Chapin's invitation years later:
"In extolling to Mr. Edmands and myself the charms of
Estes Park for mountain lovers, he held out as a special
lure the possibility of at least one virgin climb."[34]

The first days of their stay at Ferguson's were given over
to "minor walks and climbs" to nearby Prospect, Giant-

track, Rams Horn, and Lily mountains and then to longer excursions to "the Wind River Range (Estes Cone and other points south of Wind River and Aspen Brook)."[35] Fay, on his own but doubtless at Chapin's suggestion, climbed to the crest of Deer Mountain, from where he could obtain a spectacular view of Mount Ypsilon across Horseshoe Park. Other climbs followed, in which various members of the larger group alternately took part: Flattop Mountain, Chasm Lake, Longs Peak, Hagues Peak, Hallett Glacier, and Stones Peak. Then came the promised "virgin climb," a three-day excursion led by William Hallett to the summit of Ypsilon Mountain, after which Edmands and Fay descended by way of the now-familiar trail over (then unnamed) Mount Chiquita and Mount Chapin. It is these adventures of 1888 that provide the central focus of Chapin's *Mountaineering in Colorado.*

A happy, nearly idyllic summer passed all too quickly into a sad fall. On September 13, 1888, Alice Chapin died of consumption. Though she had apparently been in poor health for some time,[36] her loss affected Chapin greatly.[37] As a means of consolation, Chapin turned again to the mountains of Colorado, and prepared an account of the ascent of Mount Ypsilon for the December 1888 number of *Appalachia.* He also persuaded the leadership of the AMC to share the cost of bringing together in a single volume an expanded account of his Colorado adventures. Published under Club auspices in November of 1889, *Mountaineering in Colorado: The Peaks about Estes Park* sold well. By January 1890, sales receipts had repaid the club's initial advance of $350, and the first edition itself was soon exhausted. The William H. Clarke Company of Boston published new editions in 1892, 1893, and 1899; British editions appeared in 1890 and 1896. Interestingly enough, given the widespread interest in the subject, Chapin's *Mountaineering in Colorado* has not been republished in the twentieth century until now.

Frederick Chapin returned to Colorado in September

1889. Not surprisingly, he avoided Estes Park in favor of a visit to Mesa Verde in the extreme southwestern corner of the state. Accompanied once again by Charles P. Howard, Chapin made his way to Durango by way of Colorado Springs and Ouray, where they took the time to climb 14,110-foot Pikes Peak and 14,143-foot Mount Sneffles.[38] The timing of Chapin's arrival at Mesa Verde could not have been more fortuitous. To be sure, the existence of cliff dwellings in the more accessible canyons of the Mesa Verde had been known for some time. They had been re- ported by a number of early government reconnaissance parties, and, more recently in 1874–76, had been investi- gated by members of the Hayden Survey. Descriptive accounts of the Mancos ruins by photographer William H. Jackson and geologist William H. Holmes were included in Hayden's Reports for 1874 and 1876, and Jackson's widely circulated photographs made in 1874, 1875, and 1876 had brought the mysterious legacy of Mesa Verde to the attention of a larger public. But all that was prologue: the most important and sensational secrets of the Mesa Verde lay undisturbed in side canyons that none of the ear- lier parties had bothered to penetrate. Discovery came on December 18, 1888, less than a year before Chapin's visit, when Richard Wetherill and his brother-in-law Charlie Mason, tracking stray cattle across the top of the mesa, looked out through falling snowflakes at the ruins of sprawling Cliff Palace in the wall of the opposite canyon scarcely half a mile away.

Just how Chapin heard of the Wetherill-Mason discov- ery is unclear. What is clear is that he and Howard were among the first visitors to arrive at the Wetherill's Alamo Ranch south of Mancos, Colorado, at the edge of the mesa. Guided by Richard Wetherill, the two New Englanders spent a number of days exploring and photographing the treasures of the Mancos Canyon. Returning to Hartford, Chapin quickly (and with surprising thoroughness) re- searched the subject and by February 13, 1890, had a paper, "The Cliff-Dwellings of the Mancos Canons," ready to deliver to his Appalachian colleagues. Chapin attached enough importance to the occasion to travel to Boston to deliver personally his paper before the assembled Apalachians. As AMC minutes note, "The paper was finely illustrated by eighty stereopticon views taken by himself, that of 'The Palace' being especially striking and beautiful."[39] Publication soon followed, both in the May 1890 number of *Appalachia* and the July 1890 number of *The American Antiquarian and Oriental Journal.*[40]

This paper provided the impetus for Frederick Chapin's second book, *The Land of the Cliff-Dwellers*, which was published at Boston in 1892 by the Appalachian Mountain Club. It proved both timely and important. The "first widely distributed information on the antiquities of the Mesa Verde region,"[41] Chapin's book was subsequently praised by no less an authority than noted anthropologist Frederick W. Hodge. Writing in the January 1893 number of *The American Anthropologist*, Hodge observed that

Although the volume does not claim to be a scientific treatise, the archeologist may well rejoice in the possession of a hundred pages or more of accurate description of the vestiges of an ancient pueblo culture, which vandalism threatens soon to destroy. . . . Accompanying the descriptive text are three maps, a dozen excellent full-page heliotype engravings, besides some fifty-five halftone plates illustrative mainly of cliff villages or of various features of their architecture, pottery, basketry, etc., from the photographs by the author. The scientific value of the work will increase with its age. As a specimen of the book-maker's art it could scarcely be excelled.[42]

To Hodge's appreciation can be added the fact that one of the principal mesas of the Mesa Verde, containing the ruins known as Cliff Palace, Sprucetree House, and Bal-

Mary Hastings Potter Chapin, Frederick Chapin's second wife, ca. 1881.
Courtesy of Patricia Potter Duncan.

cony House, now bears Frederick Chapin's name.

Of the final eight years of Chapin's life we know very little. Though the anonymous sketch written at the time of his death states that he made an 1894 visit to the Himalayas of India and returned home by way of Calcutta and the Pacific Ocean,[43] little exists in the way of corroboration other than the fact that Chapin did review three recent books on Himalayan exploration for the December 1893 number of *Appalachia*.[44] Otherwise, to all appearances, Frederick Chapin lived the quiet life of a successful Hartford businessman. Leisure hours were given over to raising horses and to enjoying the solitude of the "Bungalow," the house he had built for himself in West Hartford, whose wood interior, two-story beamed living room, massive stone fireplace, and simple masculine furnishings gave it the appearance of an elegant mountainside lodge. At the age of forty-six, Frederick Chapin decided to remarry. His bride was Mary Hastings Potter (1863–1946) of Lafayette, Indiana, a second cousin, whom he had apparently come to court through the good offices of the Sisson family.[45] The wedding took place in Lafayette on November 30, 1898, after which Frederick and Mary returned to Hartford. Though their marriage was apparently a happy one, it was tragically short. Less than fourteen months later, on January 25, 1900, after a lingering illness, Frederick Chapin died of tuberculosis, leaving his wife and a five-day-old daughter.[46]

Chapin's task in writing *Mountaineering in Colorado* was not a particularly difficult one. The core of the book, some forty percent of the whole, already existed in the three papers published in *Appalachia*.[47] Of these, only Chapin's account of his 1887 ascent of Longs Peak required anything resembling major revision. In this case, Chapin simply lifted two paragraphs out of the opening section and transferred them to Chapter I ("Estes Park"), and then added to the original Longs Peak narrative the accounts of his two 1888 trips to Chasm Lake and the account of his visit to the beaver ponds. The other published *Appalachia* articles, recounting the visit to Hallett [Rowe] Glacier and the ascent of Mount Ypsilon, became, with only minor changes, Chapters V and VI. The remaining four chapters, consisting of new material, by and large follow, as Chapin notes, the chronology of the original events themselves.

As a contribution to the literature of American mountaineering, Frederick Chapin's *Mountineering in Colorado* belies its casual tone and apparent artlessness. For all the easy camaraderie that marked their excursions and monthly meetings, the founding members of the Appalachian Mountain Club took the business of mountaineering seriously. As early as the third number of *Appalachia,* the club's Exploration Committee set down a series of "directions" to guide excursionists in making observations:

> The notes taken should include:—
> (a.) A description of the trip;
> (b.) A table of the *times* of starting, stopping, arriving, etc., together with such calculations or estimates of distances, elevations, etc., as are available;
> (c.) A rough map of the route traversed.[48]

On the matter of "description," the committee's directives were precise:

> The description of the trip should embrace a clear and succinct account of the actual experiences; it should mention the names of the party; it should especially state the quantity, position, and nature, of the water found,—whether probably a permanent source, whether drinkable, etc.; it should include a general statement of the nature of the view obtained on any summit or prominent point,—whether there is a near or

a distant horizon, whether there are any peculiarities in the view, e.g., whether any two or more mountains are seen in line with each other, or whether any very distant mountains are visible; especially what portions of the horizon are cut off by any intervening object. Difficulties should be spoken of,—the presence of scrub fir, its extent and average height; the steepness or roughness of the surface, the occurrence of swamps, thick woods, large tracts of dead or fallen trees, should be noticed, etc., etc.[49]

With the exception of the requested map, Chapin's *Mountaineering in Colorado* is faithful to the club's injunctions and on those grounds alone it can claim a seminal place in Colorado's mountain literature. Yet, Chapin's book is clearly far more than a hiking and climbing guide to the peaks about Estes Park. It is a series of delightful and leisurely narrratives about old-time mountaineering, made all the more remarkable and interesting because of the close attention paid to the trail and to the topographical and geological features of the country, because of its accompanying anecdotal glimpses of mountain life, and because of its shared bits and pieces of personal, local, and regional history. Thanks to its author's descriptive ability, the larger details of Chapin's account are those with which the contemporary summer visitor can readily identify. The names and faces of one's companions change with the years; the mountains do not. Frederick Chapin's Estes Park remains in the most essential ways very much our own; and those who hike up Longs Peak this year or next could do worse than to take with them a copy of Chapin's book. After a six-mile walk they will find stretching away before them the same slab-strewn Boulderfield, and rising above it the same jagged Keyhole. Should they elect to go on, and many do not, they will climb up the same Trough, traverse the same Narrows, and, finally, somehow, find the energy to crawl up the same Home Stretch, only to look out from the summit, as Frederick Chapin did, on the spectacular scene below. That our recollection and appreciation of such experiences can be rekindled by Chapin's words and pictures, even at the full distance of a century, serves to remind us of the compelling attraction of mountains and mountaineering, even as it underscores both the literary merit and historic importance of Chapin's charming book.

In the narrative that follows Frederick Chapin has been allowed to tell his own story. As editor, I have limited myself to a series of explanatory notes, mostly topographical and historical in nature, as an aid to the modern reader.[50] I should like to use the occasion of this introduction to acknowledge and thank a number of those individuals who have responded to my queries and requests for information: Portia Allbert, Kansas State Historical Society; Lennie Bemis, Estes Park Public Library; Anne W. Borg, Kent Memorial Library, Suffield, Connecticut; Donald Brown, National Park Service, Rocky Mountain National Park; Mel Bush, Estes Park Area Historical Museum; Robin M. Carlaw, Harvard University Archives; Patricia Potter Duncan, Palo Alto, California; Catherine T. Engel, Colorado Historical Society; Nan L. Glass, town of West Hartford; Brenda Hamby, Leavenworth County Historical Society; John Hewitt, Appalachian Mountain Club, Boston; Eric L. Mundell, Indiana Historical Society; Barbara L. Neilon, Tutt Library, Colorado College; Hawley Rising, Suffield, Connecticut; Leon Stiles, Penn Yan, N.Y.; Nancy Weirich and Ann Shafer, Tippecanoe County Area Genealogical Society; Anne H. Willard, Everett C. Wilkie, Jr., and Christopher P. Bickford, Connecticut Historical Society; Brigid Welch, Helen Tatman, and Michael Gibbs, M. D. Anderson Library, University of Houston–University Park.

NOTES

1. Quoted in Dave Hicks, *Estes Park from the Beginning* (Denver: Egan Print Co. in association with A-T-P Publishing Co., 1976), p. 47.

2. Quoted in June E. Carothers, *Estes Park Past and Present* (University of Denver Press, 1951), p. 72.

3. The activities and annual reports of the Hayden Survey, which spent the summers of 1873 to 1876 exploring and mapping the state, also played a role in the popularization of Colorado. See Preface, n. 4. The history of Hayden's Colorado survey is recounted in Richard A. Bartlett, *Great Surveys of the American West* (Norman: University of Oklahoma Press, 1962), pp. 74–130.

4. Gilbert Warren Chapin, *The Chapin Book of Genealogical Data. With Brief Biographical Sketches of the Descendants of Deacon Samuel Chapin* (Hartford: Chapin Family Association, 1924), pp. 53, 195, 956, 1540.

5. 1850 Census, pp. 124, 183, typescript copy, Tippecanoe County Area Genealogical Society Library, Lafayette, Indiana. Asa Chapin (1787–1870), a native of New Jersey, married Lucy Van Horn (1783–1832) in 1810. Listed in the 1850 Census as a clerk, he remained in Lafayette in the dry goods business until at least 1858. He subsequently followed Luther to Leavenworth, where he died "at the residence of his son, L. Chapin" on August 4, 1870.

6. Quoted in Emma Lou Thornbrough, *Indiana in the Civil War Era, 1850–1880* (Indianapolis: Indiana Historical Bureau and Indiana Historical Society, 1965), p. 560.

7. Gertrude Eliza Chapin was born on September 5, 1856, and died at Hartford on June 11, 1877. The Chapins had three other children, all boys—Luther Noel, born in 1850, Ernest, born in 1853, and Walter—none of whom survived infancy.

8. Daniel R. Anthony, August 17, 1857. Edgar Langsdorf and R. W. Richmond, eds., "Letters of Daniel R. Anthony, 1857–1862," *Kansas Historical Quarterly* 24 (Spring 1958): 20. The Anthony letters, published in four installments in the Spring, Summer, Fall, and Winter 1958 issues of the *Kansas Historical*

Quarterly, provide a valuable insight into life in Leavenworth during Chapin's youth.

9. Leavenworth city directories for the years 1860–70 show that Luther Chapin worked for a succession of dry goods concerns. Between 1860 and 1862, he worked for William Fairchild & Co., in 1863 for Brant & Co., and in 1865 for C. W. Thomas & Co. In subsequent directories he is listed simply as "clerk" or "salesman" for a variety of firms.

10. Luther Chapin married Mrs. Sarah (Powell) Dodd, who had been born in Alexandria, Virginia, in 1825. At the time of Frederick's death in 1900, Luther was living in Falls Church, Virginia.

11. "Frederick H. Chapin: Sketch of Him as Traveler, Student and Writer," *Hartford Daily Courant,* January 26, 1900, p. 5. The author, who was well acquainted with Chapin and his history, may well have been Thomas Sisson (see below). This sketch appeared the day after Chapin's death and was accompanied by two tributes. The first was signed with the initials "H.C." (quite possibly for Charles P. Howard, see n. 19 below); the second by Jeremiah Mervin Allen (1833–1903), president of the Hartford Boiler Inspection Company and a leading citizen of the city.

12. Quoted in Kenneth R. Andrews, *Nook Farm: Mark Twain's Hartford Circle* (Cambridge, Mass.: Harvard University Press, 1950), p. 18.

13. Quoted in Ibid., p. 20.

14. The nineteen-room, five-bath red brick mansion that Mark Twain erected in 1874 was located at 351 Farmington Avenue.

15. Thomas Sisson, a native of West Hartford, "was the dean of druggists in the state," and at the time of his death in 1907 had been doing business at the same location — 729 Main Street in Hartford — for some sixty-eight years. *Hartford Daily Courant,* January 1, 1907, p. 4, and May 2, 1907, p. 6; Charles W. Burpee, *History of Hartford County, Connecticut, 1633–1928* (Chicago: S. J. Clarke Publishing Co., 1928), vol. 1, 479; vol. 2, 690.

16. According to an anonymous sketch, "He was always fond of reading and study, his inclination leading him rather to scientific knowledge and to works on travel and adventure. The story of Kane's Arctic explorations interested him so much when he was 10 or 11 years of age that throughout his life he was able to repeat the name of every one of Kane's officers and sailors." The allusion

is to Elisha Kent Kane, whose enormously popular *Arctic Explorations: The Second Grinnell Expedition in Search of Sir John Franklin in the Years 1853, '54, '55,* published in two volumes in 1856, was for a time to be found on American parlor tables everywhere.

17. Frederick Hastings Chapin, "Ascent of the Zinal Rothhorn," *Appalachia* 4 (July 1885): 97.

18. There are scattered references to Chapin's expeditions to the Adirondacks, including the suggestion in an anonymous sketch that he may have visited them in the company of his maternal grandfather, David Hastings (1793–1877), of nearby Suffield, Connecticut. See also n. 37, below.

19. In the Hartford *Directory for 1879,* Charles P. Howard is listed as secretary of the firm of James L. Howard & Company, which manufactured and sold railroad car furnishings. Howard would subsequently accompany Chapin on at least one of his visits to Colorado. A friend of the Sisson family as well, Charles P. Howard served as an honorary pallbearer at Mrs. Sisson's funeral in 1910.

20. Frederick H. Chapin, "Ascents of the Breithorn and Mont Blanc," *Appalachia* 5 (December 1887): 39.

21. Charles P. Howard, "An Ascent of the Matterhorn," *Lippincott's Magazine of Popular Literature and Science* 24 (September 1879): 351–59.

22. *Appalachia* 5 (December 1887): 42.

23. Ibid., 46.

24. Ibid., 50.

25. Alice Seavey was the daughter of John H. and Julia Steele Seavey. Like the family of Thomas Sisson, the Seavey family was well-represented in the nineteenth-century history of West Hartford. See, for example, William H. Hall, *West Hartford* (Hartford: West Hartford Chamber of Commerce, 1930), pp. 12, 13, 88, 130, 146, 183–84.

26. *Appalachia* 1 (June 1876): 3.

27. Ibid., 2 (May 1881): 295.

28. The proceedings of the February 9, 1887, meeting of the AMC note that "A letter from Mr. F. H. Chapin, describing his ascent of Pike's Peak, was read by Mr. F. O. Carpenter." *Appalachia,* 5 (December 1887): 83.

29. Many of the papers that Chapin presented on Colorado, and

virtually all of the published ones, were accompanied by his own photographs. In 1889 and 1890 Chapin put together six albums of his photographs, some 285 pictures in all, and presented them to the AMC for its Boston library. Chapin was also among the first Americans to take a collector's interest in (and be influenced by) the work of the celebrated Italian photographer Vittorio Sella (1859–1943). Sella's magnificent photographs of the Swiss Alps, including the Breithorn that Chapin had climbed in 1877, began to be commercially available in late 1882 or 1883. (It is just possible that the two men actually met, for both were in Switzerland during the summer of 1882.) In 1893 Chapin loaned his collection of Sella prints to the Appalachian Mountain Club as part of a May exhibition of Sella's work jointly sponsored by the AMC and the Boston Art Club. It was this exhibition that first brought Sella to the attention of the American public and encouraged the Appalachian Mountain Club to launch a subscription campaign, the Sella Fund (chaired by Professor Charles Fay), to establish for its library a permanent collection of his prints. See *Appalachia* 7 (March 1894): 229, and Ronald Clark, *The Splendid Hills: The Life and Photographs of Vittorio Sella* (London: Phoenix House, 1948), pp. 23–24.

30. For an account of popular photography in the years immediately following the introduction of the commercial dry plate see F. C. Beach, "Modern Amateur Photography," *Harper's New Monthly Magazine* 78 (January 1889): 288–97. See also Robert A. Taft, *Photography and the American Scene: A Social History, 1839–1889* (New York: Dover Publications, Inc., 1964), pp. 361–83.

31. The conjecture is based on an anecdote told by Mrs. William E. James, one of Estes Park's earliest settlers. William James had originally planned to pursue the cattle business. "But every summer," as their daughter Eleanor recalled,

> people came to the ranch and begged to stay, and each winter another cabin would be built on the ranch to house them. Father and Mother soon found there was more money in caring for summer tourists than in raising cattle. Mother told the story about Mr. Chapin for whom Mt. Chapin was named. He was a guest one summer, and occupied one of the little bed-

rooms. He always kept his window open, and every day a hen would come in through the window and lay an egg on his bed.

Eleanor E. Hondius, *Memoirs of Eleanor E. Hondius of Elkhorn Lodge* (Boulder: Pruett Press, 1964), p. 7. Assuming the accuracy of the story, the circumstances suggest that Chapin's visit occurred during the summer of 1886.

32. Frederick H. Chapin, *Mountaineering in Colorado: The Peaks about Estes Park* (Boston: Appalachian Mountain Club, 1889), p. 30.

33. On the way to Estes Park, Chapin made an unsuccessful attempt to climb 14,363-foot Sierra Blanca, overlooking the San Luis Valley near Fort Garland in southeastern Colorado. His guide was none other than William Carson (1852–89), son of the celebrated trapper and guide Kit Carson. Chapin recounted his trip in a brief article ("A Trip to Sierra Blanca") published in the December 1888 number of *Appalachia* (5: 239–42).

34. Charles E. Fay, "Professor Fay Recounts Visit to Rocky Mountains in 1888," *Estes Park Trail* 6 (July 23, 1926): 3.

35. Ibid.

36. Fay, in the article cited above, describes her as an invalid, and her death certificate indicates that she had been suffering from consumption for two years.

37. Alice Chapin, despite her illness, shared her husband's love of the wilderness. The following poignant entry in the AMC minutes for December 19, 1888: "Several letters of botanical interest, written by Mrs. F. H. Chapin, from the Adirondacks, were read by Miss J. C. Clarke. Professor C. E. Fay followed with some interesting remarks concerning the writer of the letters, whose decease took place in December last." *Appalachia* 5 (May 1889): 354.

38. Frederick H. Chapin, "The San Juan Mountains," *Appalachia* 6 (December 1890): 147–62. Chapin later incorporated this account into *The Land of the Cliff-Dwellers,* where it appears as Chapter VIII.

39. *Appalachia* 6 (May 1890): 104.

40. Frederick H. Chapin, "The Cliff-Dwellings of the Mancos Canon," *Appalachia* 6 (May 1890): 12–34; *The American Antiquarian and Oriental Journal* 11 (July 1890): 193–210.

41. David A. Breternitz, "Mesa Verde National Park: A History of Its Archaeology," *Essays and Monographs in Colorado History,* n. 2 (Denver: Colorado Historical Society, 1983), p. 225.

42. Frederick W. Hodge, *The American Anthropologist* 6 (January 1893): 101.

43. Since virtually every other assertion made by the anonymous writer of this sketch of Frederick Chapin's life can be independently validated, the temptation to accept the fact of his visit to the Himalayas is great. On the other hand, Chapin's custom had been to write up his mountain experiences for his fellow Appalachians (and for *Appalachia*) almost immediately, and it is hard to believe he would have passed up the opportunity to report on a trip to an area of the world that in 1894 was remote, wild, and as yet largely unexplored.

44. *Appalachia* 7 (December 1893): 166–68.

45. Mary Hastings Potter was the daughter of Sabra and William A. Potter of Lafayette. Her mother, whose maiden name was Sabra Eliza Stiles, was the first cousin of both Chapin's mother and his aunt, Mrs. Gertrude Sissons. The ancestral home of both the Hastings and Stiles families was Suffield, Connecticut, north of Hartford, and Mary was apparently in the habit of periodically visiting her relatives. According to her account book, kindly loaned the editor by Mrs. Patricia Potter Duncan, Mary visited Hartford in 1895. Though Chapin may have first encountered Mary Potter as an adult on this occasion, it is also clear that he had kept in personal contact with the Potter family in Lafayette over the years. For example, he dutifully inscribed a copy of *Mountaineering in Colorado* "To Emily Potter [Mary's older sister] from Frederick H. Chapin December 9, 1889." The Hastings family traced its Suffield origins to Joseph Hastings (1703–85), a carpenter by trade who came to Suffield about 1726. In 1769, Joseph Hastings founded, organized, and became the first pastor of the First Baptist Church of Suffield, whose church house was erected on Zion's Hill (or Hastings Hill as it became known) to the west of town, where the family home lot and farm was also located. Members of both the Hastings and Stiles families are buried in the cemetery on Hastings Hill. The house built by Chapin's great grandfather, David Hastings (1758–1824), was located farther west at the corner of Colson and Stone streets.

46. The daughter was named Mary Hastings Chapin (1900–1968). Mary Chapin remained in Hartford until after the death of Gertrude Sisson in 1910, and then returned with her daughter to Lafayette where she could be near the Potter family. She built a small Dutch colonial house for herself and Mary, who never married, at 510 South 10th Street, and took an active interest in local activities. One of those activities was the Current Topic Club, for which Mary Chapin wrote a delightful reminiscence of her Lafayette girlhood, entitled "I Remember When." Dated January 23, 1939, it is part of the archives of the Tippecanoe County Area Genealogical Society.

47. There may have been a fourth and unpublished source for Chapin's book, for AMC minutes note that on February 3, 1888, "Mr. F. H. Chapin read a paper entitled 'Ascents in the Front Range, Colorado.' About sixty stereopicon views from Mr. Chapin's negatives were shown, illustrating scenery near Pike's Peak and in Estes Park, and especially the precipice on Long's Peak and the Hallett Glacier on Mummy Mountain." *Appalachia* 5 (June 1888): 169.

48. Ibid., 1 (June 1877): 191.

49. Ibid. Chapin himself was well aware of the requirements of the genre. "Lest the general reader should be disturbed by the personalities of the narrative," he concluded the Preface to *Mountaineering in Colorado,* "the author would remind him that the style is one customary in the large and increasing literature of mountaineering."

50. In matters concerning mountain nomenclature, spelling, and altitudes I have been guided by Louisa Ward Arps and Elinor Eppich Kingery's invaluable *High Country Names: Rocky Mountain National Park* (Estes Park, Co.: Rocky Mountain Nature Association, 1972). I have not altered Chapin's text, even though such practices as adding an apostrophe to the names of mountains causes unnecessary confusion (e.g., Long's Peak).

MOUNTAINEERING IN COLORADO

The Peaks About Estes Park

BY

FREDERICK H. CHAPIN

———◆———

BOSTON

APPALACHIAN MOUNTAIN CLUB

1889

To the Memory

OF

A. L. S. C.

WHO WAS A LOVER OF THE MOUNTAINS AND OF ALL THAT IS
BEAUTIFUL AMONG THEM, AND WHOSE COMPANIONSHIP
INSPIRED THIS VOLUME.

CONTENTS.

APPENDIX.

LIST OF ILLUSTRATIONS.

ℜlates.

𝔓rinteⅾ 𝔴it𝔥 t𝔥e 𝔗ext.

DEER MOUNTAIN FROM FERGUSON'S RANCH.

PREFACE.

———◆———

THE day for making striking discoveries in the Rocky Mountains is past. It is now three centuries and more, since Alvaro Cabeça de Vaca with three followers traversed the continent from the Gulf of Mexico to the Spanish settlements on the Pacific coast. His wanderings led him through the region now known as New Mexico; thus he beheld and crossed the southern Rockies. Nearly a hundred and fifty years later, two French explorers, the brothers La Vérendrye, crossed the prairies from the great lakes, and, reaching a point near the sources of the Yellowstone River, were the first white men to look upon the northern peaks. Since the day of these early adventurers the exploring parties of Lewis and Clark, Pike, Long, and Fremont have opened the way; and more recently the better equipped expeditions of Hayden, Powell, King, and others have explored the sierras and cañons, especially those of Colorado.

There remain only byways and corners to be
more thoroughly searched; and fortunate will be
the adventurer who finds anything of note that
has not already been seen and written about by
the indefatigable members of survey parties that
have preceded him.

But in climbing some of the peaks in the autumn of 1886 I saw much that was novel, and
during succeeding seasons other remarkable sights
forced themselves, as it were, right before my
camera.   Mr. Ferguson, a pioneer of '59, at whose
ranch I stayed while in Estes Park, told me, on
the day of my leaving, " I reckon no man ever
came into this Park before, and saw as much as
you have seen." Some of the success which was
attained in certain carefully planned expeditions
was due to luck; more must be placed to the
credit of the clear skies and continual sunshine
of Colorado.

Though I have made many ascents in other
parts of the Rocky Mountains, the peaks most
thoroughly explored are those that surround Estes
Park ; for this reason it has been decided to limit
the present descriptions to these northern peaks.
The earlier ascents have proved very useful, however, in enabling me to identify different points
seen in extended mountain views.

It will be noticed that on several occasions we added to the nomenclature of the range; this, however, was done only in cases where we felt compelled to have a name for mountain or snow-field. Wherever an expedition is recorded as new, the claim is made on the authority of the frontiersmen who have lived longest in the mountains.

With the exception of records of second expeditions on the same mountain, the narrative follows the order of the dates of the ascents.

Upon the illustrations depends much of the interest of the book. With but few exceptions they are made directly from negatives taken in my various expeditions. They cost hard work and great care; to obtain them our packs were often heavy. The reproductions were made by the Boston Photogravure Company.

Parts of the chapters on Long's Peak, Mummy Mountain, and Ypsilon Peak were originally printed in "Appalachia," the journal of the Appalachian Mountain Club; and certain episodes related in Chapters II. and VII. appeared in "Scribner's Magazine" for February, 1889. I am under great obligations to Messrs. Charles Scribner's Sons for their kind permission to print certain pages, and also for the use of their engraving "Photographing the Big-horn," which

accompanied the original text. It has been reduced by a photographic process.

It is believed that the catalogue of the flora of
Estes Park, printed as an appendix, will be of interest to many who visit the Rockies. The speci-
mens named were for the most part collected by
my wife during her two summers' residence in
the Park. Coulter's "Manual of the Botany of
the Rocky Mountain Region" is the authority followed. The list has been revised and extended by
Mrs. George W. Thacher, an indefatigable botanist
and an ardent lover of Colorado's mountains.

It is very flattering to me that the Appalachian
Mountain Club, for whose members many of the
articles forming this volume were primarily written,
should have deemed them worthy of publication
under its auspices. Lest the general reader should
be disturbed by the personalities of the narrative,
the author would remind him that the style is one
customary in the large and increasing literature of
mountaineering.

MOUNTAINEERING IN COLORADO.

CHAPTER I.

ESTES PARK.

THE mighty ranges of the Rockies come sweeping down from the north, through Montana and northern Wyoming, as several nearly parallel ranges, occupying a great breadth of country, in some sections as much as four hundred miles. South of Fremont's Peak the several ranges give place to a high plateau, over which the Union Pacific Railroad finds a way from Cheyenne westward. From this plateau the mountains rise again to great heights and enter central Colorado as two distinct ranges, — the Medicine Bow Mountains on the east, and the Park Range farther to the west. The Front Range, so called from its geographical position, rises abruptly from the plains in northern Colorado, and is marked by such lofty summits as Hague's Peak (13,832 feet) and Long's Peak (14,271 feet), in the north, and Pike's Peak (14,147 feet), near the end of the range, a hundred miles farther south. Then comes a break in the chain, where the Arkansas River flows through deep cañons on its journey to the plains. South of this break the Wet River Mountains and the Sangre de Cristo Range mark the eastern borders of the Rockies of Colorado.

Standing upon some high peak in the centre of the great ranges that front on the plains, one sees, a hundred miles away toward the New Mexico line, that noble peak of the southern Rockies, Sierra Blanca. In the opposite direction, one hundred miles to the north, towers Long's Peak, its mighty mass dwarfing all other mountains near it. To reach Sierra Blanca, the traveller ascends by the famous railway, with its mule-shoe curve, over Veta Pass, through scenery of world-renowned grandeur; but if he will climb the slopes of Blanca Peak to timber-line, he will behold scenery that will for the moment almost obliterate from his mind the fact that there is such a place as Veta Pass.

To reach the vales near Long's Peak, the old stage-coach must serve the tourists' purpose. The narrow-gauge line of the Denver, Utah, and Pacific Railroad, now a link in the great Burlington sys-

tem, lands him at Lyons, the last station on the
plains, at the base of the range, and a stage-
ride of thirty miles brings him to the beautiful
valley of Estes Park. Here, too, as in San Luis
Park and in the neighborhood of Sierra Blanca,
remarkable as are the valleys and foot-hills, there
are scenes among the mountain tops which far
surpass in beauty and sublimity any of those
viewed along the railway or stage lines. To ap-
preciate the wonders of the sierras, one must
climb among them.

Estes Park, in which are many picturesque
scenes, is the natural centre for mountaineering in
northern Colorado. It is situated near the Wyoming line, and about seventy miles northwest of
Denver. Its elevation is about seven thousand
feet above the sea. There are about ten thousand
acres of pasture-land bordering the banks of the
Big Thompson Creek and the smaller streams, and
these have all been taken up as homestead claims
by pioneers. Seven thousand acres have passed
into the hands of an English company, which, I
was informed, were originally intended for a great
game preserve, but the ranch interests are now
predominant, and large herds of cattle of graded
Hereford breeds roam through the pastures. Besides the ranch of the English company, — which

owns a small hotel here, — there are five other ranches in the Park; and at one of these, Ferguson's, we made our headquarters for two seasons.

The early history of Estes Park has been told; but the place is so little visited, except by the dwellers on the plains near the foot-hills, that a few words describing its present condition and its settlement may be of interest.

The precious metals not being found in this region, no railway winds through the cañon of the St. Vrain, nor through the rough Muggin's Gulch. The whistle of the locomotive is never heard in the valley; and except that, instead of the primitive elk and deer, a few cattle roam through the pastures, and that an occasional wire fence closes the narrow entrance from one valley to another, little is changed from the original aspect of the country.

Mr. Lamb, who lives at the immediate base of Long's Peak, settled there in 1876. Mr. Ferguson came into the valley some fourteen years ago. Originally from Missouri, he was a pioneer of '59, crossed the plains with an ox-team, and settled in the lowlands of Colorado; but he was unfortunate in having his crops destroyed by grasshoppers. He came up into the mountains prospecting, and from the Loveland divide had his

Ferguson's Ranch.

first look at Estes Park. He quickly made up his mind to settle in it. He still tells, with a glow of enthusiasm, of his first view of the valley. Even after taking up his claim in this out-of-the-way place, he was troubled again by the insect that had caused his first great loss; but observing the approach of the pest up through the narrow glade that leads from Estes Park to his higher claim, he felled timber, made a barricade, set fire to it, and saved his crops. His ranch is delight-fully situated, and, though a mile from the river, is supplied with cold clear water from a never-failing spring. From the cabins around Ferguson's ranch a magnificent view is obtained of the great Mummy Range; and the sunset lights on the cliffs of Lily Mountain, to the east, are inde-scribably beautiful. Especially is this true during the waning of the rainy season, if the slight rain-falls of June and July can be so called. The mornings during this season are clear and beauti-ful; but in the early afternoon the great peak of the Mummy will perhaps throw off its cloud streamer, and in an hour or two thunder will rattle among the crags of Sheep Mountain, and the rain pour down upon the dry pastures. In a few hours the sun almost gains the mastery once more; and though the pine-belts and valleys may be covered with ascending vapors, the peak of Lily will glow with gorgeous hues. It is probably some such spectacle as this that makes one of the early writers about this valley claim for it the finest scenery in the world. This statement is hardly justified, for we cannot apply to the surrounding mountains, however beautiful they may be, the words of Hiouen Tsang in describing a Himalayan view : " The top of the mountain rises to the sky." * Yet Long's Peak, with its great altitude, is truly a cloud-piercer. Like Mount Hood, which has probably gone up and down in the scale of estimated heights more than any other mountain in the West, its stated altitude has been subject to marked variation. It was given in 1857 as 15,000 feet, in 1879 as 14,700, while its present accepted elevation is 14,271 feet.

Near by Ferguson's is Mary's Lake, a little sheet of alkaline water, Lily Mountain rising on the south, Sheep Mountain on the west, and Prospect Mountain on the east. It was formerly a great resort for big-horn, elk, and deer, which came in great numbers to the lake, as they would to a salt-lick; and many have been shot there. Mr. Ferguson told how in those days, when hunted

* Quoted by Andrew Wilson, Abode of Snow, p. 274 : Putnam, 1875.

near the lake, the big-horn would scramble up the steep isolated ledges which rise out of the open country to a height of one or two hundred feet. They were then easily surrounded, and escape from rifle-armed hunters was impossible. This, however, was in the early days of the country's

settlement, and before the big-horn had learned the ways of hunters.

This very wild animal is undoubtedly the rarest and most interesting game found in the Rocky Mountains of Wyoming and Colorado.* Hunters and ranchmen assured me that it had entirely

---

* The accompanying illustration of the head of a young ram is made from an animal which Mr. Ferguson shot on the banks of Mary's lake. The circumference of the horns in the illustration, at the base next the head, is thirteen and three-fourths inches ; length of horn, nineteen and a half inches.

forsaken the Front Range, and was to be found only in the mountains beyond North Park, or in Wyoming; but I was able to prove it otherwise. The higher sierras retain all their primeval wildness. Many of the peaks in the Front and Rabbit Ear Ranges remain unscaled, cañons among them are still unexplored, and dark forests which fill the upper valleys have never known the foot of man; so that the chance which the explorer runs of meeting with rare wild animals, sometimes of a ferocious type, makes mountaineering in the Rockies more exciting than in the older countries.

Aside from the deer, which are numerous, the most common large animal in Estes Park is probably the bear. The brown and cinnamon bear are the species generally met with. I am informed that there is perhaps no real difference between the two, for when a litter of cubs is found, some of the young ones are black and some are brown. Grizzlies are rarely seen; but it is related by ranchmen in Estes Park that during the summer of 1886 one made himself quite at home in the valley, and one night while wandering around killed several full-grown steers. Lamb, the guide to Long's Peak, says that he saw his tracks many times. A mountain lion was seen at Sprague's ranch during the early winter of the same year, coolly prowling around and among the log-cabins.

Near Timber-line on Sprague's Trail.

As before stated, the principal visitors in this upland valley are from the low regions of Larimer County. Many of them bring tents and cooking utensils, and camp by the Big Thompson or the St. Vrain Rivers. The visitors at the ranches are from Denver and far eastern towns.

Trout-fishing is the principal sport. Hunters are more attracted to the North Park, which one

may reach by Cameron's Pass.   The lover of
high mountain ascents finds a good field for
novel expeditions throughout the range; for,
with the exception of Long's Peak, the high
elevations are rarely visited.

Some of these objective points are visible from
Ferguson's Ranch; one has but to take a half-
hour's stroll on Sheep Mountain near at hand, to
behold a long line of noble peaks from a point
where Albert Bierstadt made many studies for
one of his great pictures.

CHAPTER II.

I.

L ONG'S PEAK is of great interest to the mountaineer. It is the highest point in northern Colorado, and its ascent is more difficult than that of any other peak in the range. It has been rather fancifully named the "American Matterhorn;" but when we consider that one side is actually inaccessible, perhaps it is worthy the comparison, — for the Matterhorn has been ascended by *arêtes* on all sides, though, of course, its easiest line of ascent is manifold harder to conquer than is the ordinary route of Long's Peak.

Before narrating our experiences on Long's Peak itself, perhaps it would be well to speak of several views of the mountain from points in and around Estes Park. One thing very noticeable is the fact that the mountain presents so widely different aspects when seen from the four points of the compass. From the plains to the southeast, two

SUMMIT OF LONG'S PEAK OVER CRAGS OF MOUNT HALLETT.

noble peaks appear as if of nearly equal altitude.
From the top of Sheep Mountain, — a long range
(9,000 feet) near Ferguson's ranch,—the final cone,
only five miles away, demonstrates its superior-
ity, and grandly lifts its head over the intervening
wooded slopes of Estes Cone. Wind River Valley, which lies between Sheep Mountain and the
main range, is 2,000 feet lower than Sheep Mountain; so from this elevation one may behold a
slope of 7,000 feet leading up to the summit of
the principal peak. Still more majestic is its
appearance from the top of Prospect Mountain,
eight miles distant and overlooking Sheep Mountain, which is then projected against the base of
the great range. But by far the most striking
view is that obtained from Table Mountain, a
peak on the Continental divide, about six miles to
the northwest. I imagine that very few persons
have beheld Long's Peak from this direction; and
the photograph from which the illustration that
precedes this chapter was made, cost me many
hours of climbing and much setting up of the
camera and experimenting before this most characteristic view was obtained. The appearance of
the noble mountain is like a citadel perched upon
enormous bastions and protected by ramparts
made by intervening walls of rock.

Mountaineers may realize, from examination of this illustration, what a splendid field it is for new expeditions, — either to follow the summit of the chain along the spur to the right, or to explore the upper cañons and glacial lakelets. The numerous lakes among these gorges add greatly to the picturesqueness of the views. A summer spent among these rock walls would present any number of varying excursions which would show to the explorer marvellous and enjoyable sights, with the bare possibility that he might find something that would add to our stock of knowledge. Members of foreign alpine clubs have thoroughly explored and photographed the ice districts of Switzerland, and partially so the Caucasus; but the noble work of the survey parties in the sierras of Colorado has not yet been supplemented to any great extent by individual effort. The same work remains to be done among the higher elevations of the whole great chain reaching from New Mexico to Alaska, that has been done by European alpine clubs in Switzerland, and is being marked out by the Appalachian Mountain Club in New England. Paths are to be made, trails to be cut, detail maps to be laid out, before the grandest scenes among the mountains can be shown to the tourist.

It is a rare occurrence in Estes Park to have
four successive rainy days; but so it happened in
the summer of 1887, from July 14 to 17. The
season, however, had been very dry, and the
parched ground needed the deluge which it received. The sun appeared at intervals during
each of these days, but it would soon be hidden
and the storm would continue. We had set several times for an attack on Long's Peak ; but the
weather had put us back, and we knew, from the
whitened appearance of Mummy Mountain, that
much snow was falling.on the great range. At
last, however, on Monday, July 18, we had a clear
day, and made arrangements to start in the afternoon for Lamb's ranch, — which is situated at the
base of the peak, — there to spend the night, and
in the morning make an attempt to gain the desired summit. There were four of us in the party;
and two of the number left Ferguson's at five
o'clock, while with one companion I rode over
after tea, arriving at Lamb's at eight.

Even this part of the expedition is full of interest. The road skirts the side of Mary's Lake, and
leads through wide pastures for the first two miles ;
then passes up a steep hill, through a forest, with
the stupendous cliffs of Lily Mountain hanging
over the valley. This mountain is 11,453 feet in

height above sea-level, and its summit corresponds
with the average of timber-line on the great range.
The upper cliffs are steep and bare on the inner
side, while on the eastern side, which is a gradual
slope, heavy timber grows to the top; hence from
the plains the mountain has an entirely different
appearance, showing two black summits, and is
called by another name, "The Twin Sisters."
Lily Lake, quite a large expanse of water, lies at
the base of the mountain, and gives it its name.
As we passed the lake, we saw several mallard
ducks on its surface.

Our host, Mr. Ferguson, tells this story : Many
years ago, with one companion, he was shooting on
the edge of this lake.   They discharged their guns
into a flock of mallards which were out on the
water, but with no other effect than to cause the
frightened ducks to fly over Sheep Mountain to
another lake.   Very soon he noticed them returning in his direction, and two of them flying in a
straight line at as rapid a rate as possible, while
the others bore away down the valley.   The fore-
most bird struck the lake in the centre, and dived
out of sight; and then Mr. Ferguson saw that the
one following was a very large eagle, which, foiled
in the pursuit, soared into a tree and alighted
there.   The hunters now emptied barrel after

barrel at the duck ; but they could not frighten it
out of the lake, where it remained until they finally
killed it. The eagle, of course, escaped.

Lamb's claim is in a high, well-watered valley ;
in fact, it is al-
most a swamp in
some places.
The elevation
is about 8,500
feet above the
sea, making it
about 1000
feet above
Ferguson's
ranch. Mr.
Lamb senior
took up a
homestead
claim here,
some ten years
ago, and for
many years
guided travel-

Long's Peak from Lamb's Ranch.

lers up the peak; but for the past three years
his son Carlyle has done this work, and had already ascended fifty-five times at the date of
our visit. He is a strong, willing guide ; and

he worked very hard for me, for our packs were heavy. Until my acquaintance with him began, he had never climbed any of the elevations west of Long's Peak. Lamb keeps a charming mountain-inn; the house, which is built of logs, is very comfortable, and our advance guard announced that they had been served to a remarkably good supper. All the supplies which he purchases he has to haul up from the plains, thirty miles distant. In the sitting-room of the house is a very large fireplace, made of rough stones, before which, while the logs were crackling and blazing, we sat till late in the evening, talking of the mountains; and when we did turn in, I did not go to sleep till after twelve, and was awake at three o'clock.

Perhaps the stories of our host had something to do with it; for the elder Lamb tells some very interesting ones of his many ascents of the mountain, the most exciting of which, without doubt, was that made in company with Mr. Sylvester C. Dunham, of Hartford, Conn., an account of which was published in the magazine "Good Company," April, 1881. Mr. Lamb's account of that day's adventure is a thrilling one, and Mr. Dunham's is equally so. When upon the summit of the peak, they were enshrouded in clouds; the

early morning had been clear, and the distant
views grand; but a storm gathered on Mummy
Mountain, and swept over the great range, culmi-
nating as an electric storm on Long's Peak. In
Mr. Dunham's words, the cairn on the summit —

"hissed and crackled like a bonfire. We had sought
it as affording shelter from the approaching storm, but
we retired from its vicinity in a very informal manner.
The cloud had now struck the base of the horn, and
came boiling and rolling up the 'Trough.' Its advance guard of hard, sharp pellets of ice flew straight
up the face of the cliff, and in another minute we
were in the midst of the tempest, — a whirling volley
of ice and snow, driven by an icy blast. Little points
of white light danced in the air and beamed from
points of the rocks; and muttering thunder, of which
neither distance nor direction could be determined,
accompanied the storm."

In speaking of the electrical effects, Mr. Dunham further states: —

"My own occupation [of a cavern] was attended
by a violent shock, which fully convinced me that my
head was burned bare as a potato. Only by the immediate investigation and the earnest assurances of
my friends, was I convinced of my delusion. . . .
After some minutes the iron-bound peak seemed to
exhaust the energy of the subtle fluid wherewith the
cloud was charged; and although the tempest con-

tinued with unabated fury, we had no longer to fear the weird and mysterious element which had surrounded us. We were still in the midst of a furious storm, but it was no longer a thunder-cloud in angry combat with opposing forces."

The snow-storm was so severe that Mr. Dunham and Mr. Lamb had many uncomfortable experiences before they reached the ranch at night; but that with electrical phenomena was, of itself, such as to make their ascent more worthy of note than any other expedition to the peak.

At four o'clock the following morning we had breakfast, consisting of ham and eggs, coffee and gems; and at 5.05 o'clock were on our way over the trail. The sky was cloudy, but the peak was clear. We rode up through spruce timber for about half an hour, and then through pines, where it was much steeper, and along the banks of a little torrent which runs down to the St. Vrain River. Until within a year this route has been the only one up the mountain; but lately a trail has been cut from Sprague's ranch at Willow Park, which joins Lamb's trail at the "Bowlder Field," though it is little used. We emerged above timber-line at 6.20 o'clock, and here were met by a snow-squall. However, the clouds were light, and a brisk westerly wind began to disperse them. As we rode over the pasture-land, the sun almost broke through the vapor, and our hopes of a clear day were considerably brightened. The plains were free from haze, and all the foot-hills were sharp and clear.

I speak of this part of the trail as leading through pastures, and it certainly is a splendid grass country. Much more rain falls here than in the valleys, and the soil is moist and rich. The cattle, however, never go above the timber; and as the deer, big-horn, and elk have forsaken this mountain for the northwestern peaks, this sweet feed seems to go a-begging. The average altitude of timber growth on the northern slopes of the mountains is only a little above 11,000 feet, while on the southern side it is as much as 12,000 feet, especially where it can follow the water-courses.

We reached the edge of what is called the "Bowlder Field" at 7.30 A. M., and there tethered the horses in good grass and near plenty of water. At 7.45 we began the hard walk to the "Keyhole," — a cleft in the wall of the mountain, through which one must pass in order to climb the high peak from the west side, as the east face is inaccessible. The finest view of the great cliffs of the peak is obtained just before reaching the

"Key-hole." The face of the centre of the mountain is one nearly vertical wall of about 2,000
feet. There are but few so-called "precipices,"
even in Switzerland, which prove to be really
worth the name when closely examined; but
these walls are truly perpendicular from a point

about two hundred feet from the summit to a
gorge far below the ridge which hides the base of
the precipice. I shall refer to this marvellous
wall again when relating the story of our descent.

At 8.40 A. M. we were standing in the "Key-
hole," having made fairly quick time, considering

the delays occasioned by my having a camera along. Lamb carried my twelve sensitized plates and our lunch, while I carried the camera. I mounted it on the tripod when we left the horses, and had no serious trouble with it the whole day. In fact, there were but two places on the mountain where, while I climbed or descended, I had to hand the instrument up or down to the guide. At the "Key-hole" one looks down upon a grand amphitheatre, lying beyond the ridge just climbed. Over a deep gorge rises a mountain wall which hides the distance; and the vapor rolling up from the depths was continually changing and lifting, adding to the grandeur of the scene. No signs of animal or vegetable life were visible. Several lakes lay in the bottom of the gorge, or at the base of snow-fields on the opposite mountain.

The difficulties of the ascent of Long's Peak are frequently exaggerated. There is hardly a place on the mountain where the climber need use more than one hand to help himself up. About one hundred people have been upon the mountain annually for several years past; but this large number is made by parties, sometimes as many as twenty, coming up from Longmont or some town by the foot-hills, and all going up at once, — or trying to go up, for Lamb says that

many of them do not get beyond the " Key-hole."
Many claim to be exhausted and out of breath,
and lay it to the rarity of the air, but as most of
these people are not in training for mountain
climbing, this is not surprising: the same persons
would probably fail in undertaking a similar walk
at a lower elevation.

Immediately after leaving the " Key-hole," the
ledge traversed is quite narrow, and if one should
be very clumsy or careless and slip, a fall would
probably be fatal, — for the rocks are placed at a
very steep angle, and there is nothing to prevent
a slide of at least a thousand feet to the gorge
below.   Yet the narrow table which runs around
this side of the mountain is, on an average, about
six feet in width, and there are good footing and
flat surfaces of rock to step on; so there is not the
least danger unless one should be dizzy.   There
have been no accidents on this mountain; although one death has occurred just below the
" Key-hole," the result of over-exertion and utter
exhaustion.

From the ledges we entered the " Trough,"
which is a deep gully running up between the
main peak and a ridge of the mountain, on the
right.   This gully is quite steep, but free from
snow and ice, although there is a large field of

View from the "Trough."

snow on its side and base. There is a great deal
of loose rock and debris strewn through it, and to
traverse it is a good pull, but there is no actual
climbing: it is simply a long walk. The mountain wall ascending on the right is very smooth
and steep, but on the left the arête of the main peak
is broken up into beautiful ledges, towers, and
minarets; and as the rising vapors whirled and
rushed over them, now covering and then partly or
entirely exposing the cliffs, the effect was wonderful.
From the table-ledges we had been able to look
down 2,000 feet upon the lakes and upon a little
stream which is one of the fountain-heads of the
rushing Big Thompson River; but from this curving trough the view was upon the distant snow-
ranges.

We reached the top of the "Trough" at 10.15.
Here the plains and the mountains above Boulder
Cañon come into the prospect; but the most remarkable sight is the view of some wonderful
columnar cliffs on the southeast spur of the peak.
The upright shafts, though not detached from the
face of the cliff, are cubical on their outer surface,
and seem to be exactly perpendicular. The rocks
on the other portions of this spur, which seem not
to be so firm in texture and not tipped to vertical
position, are more easily wasted and worn away

by aerial forces; and this probably explains the
formation of the long jagged *aréte*, seen to the
right of the tower in the frontispiece. This *aréte* is
but one of the many broken ridges of the peak.

After a short rest we climbed the roof of the
peak, and at 10.50 stood upon the summit, — a
large flat surface, composed of slabs of granite.
It needs evidently only
a pyramidal cap of a

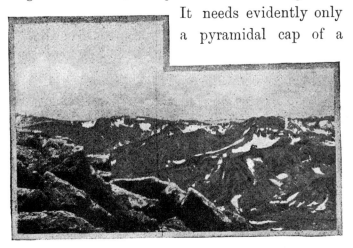

View from Long's Peak Westward.

thousand feet, to make it an ideal summit. All
was clear to the east; we could see the smoke
from the smelters of Denver, and, far beyond, the
parched plains, — the most extensive view I have
ever had in that direction. The great range of
Pike's Peak, a hundred miles to the south of us,
was so clear that I could recognize three differ-

ent summits in the chain, that I had ascended.
Cheyenne Mountain, the eastern spur of Pike's
Peak, was a landmark on the edge of the plains.
We could see the bluffs east of the town of Cheyenne, far in the north ; and towards the west
there were wonderful cloud effects over the great
ranges.

Some snow and hail now fell on the summit,
and we had to be content to await the clearing of
the storm, and meanwhile study the view and
landscape in the east and trace the course of
rivers on the plains. But even when the clouds
were thickest in the west, there would be open-
ings which would let us look into deep gorges, or
show us some peak in the Rabbit Ear Range in the
west, or the Medicine Bow group, the mighty
range of mountains in the northwest. Our most
distant view was far away to the snow-caps in
Wyoming. I looked down over one low divide
where Lamb pointed out trees growing on the
Pacific slope. While the west was obscured, we
spent some time gazing into the crater-like basin
on the east peak, the sides of which are smooth
and steep, but not as abrupt as the face of the
peak we stood upon.

For a while we thought we should have no
clear views of the western peaks ; so I set up

the camera at the west end of the summit, and
took two pictures of the partly exposed ranges,
to secure something in the way of a view from
the top, even though it should be a cloud scene;
for I feared the storm would grow fiercer, and
the mist envelop our peak for the rest of the
day. But soon the wind drove the covering from
the Front Range, and Middle Park, with Grand
River cutting a clear line through it, and all the
snow mountains which encircled the high valley,
were plainly shown to our expectant eyes. Then,
as we waited, the high pile of cloud, with its
lower fold resting on the range, was driven to the
southeast, and the peaks — Gray, Torrey, and the
Mountain of the Holy Cross — gradually appeared; and with the exception of the great mass
of Mummy Mountain, we had secured a complete
view of all the peaks and ranges ever visible from
this famous elevation. A long streamer of cloud
stretched away from the top of the Mummy
(which is the next peak in height to Long's Peak,
in this district); but it held fast to the summit,
and refused to reveal the crest of the mountain.
The Elk, Rabbit Ear, and Medicine Bow ranges
were now clear. Estes Park lay spread out like
a quiet green pasture, and Willow Cañon made a
deep black cut up through the mountains to the

northwest, towards the Medicine Bow Range. A long snow-line marked those mountains.

We reluctantly left the top at one o'clock, having remained there two hours. The outlook facing us going down the "Trough" was grand; the smooth surface of the rocks now on our right, and the towers and broken ridge on our left, made a magnificent frame through which to view the distant ranges. In this gully Lamb had a fall, and for a moment I was dazed at seeing my much-prized plates spinning in the air; but luckily there was nothing damaged, as I found, much to my wonderment, when I unpacked at night.

The "Key-hole" was gained at 2.10 P. M.; and then we followed down the "Bowlder Field" under the stupendous precipices of the peak. On this field, covering perhaps a hundred acres, are strewn great slabs of granite, — some as much as twenty feet in width and thirty feet in length, — and between them are heaped bowlders, great and small. These rocks must have been levelled by the action of frost, which split them from the once higher ridges, and left them here in past ages, in the days when Long's Peak may have had the hypothetical cap¹ which I have desired for it. Even now this great mountain shows signs of disintegration; the northern precipice is scarred and worn, and seamed with enormous cracks; slabs are loosened from its cliffs, and hang, to all appearance, like thin pieces of slate from its sides. But all the despoiling of the mountain, upon this face, is by vertical cleavage; and there are no changes going on that will destroy the absolute precipice which now exists.*

I have already referred to precipices and so-called precipices. It is probably true that Americans are more familiar with the Alps than with the Rocky Mountains; for the high valleys of Switzerland are so easy of access, and the distances are so small, that one can cross many glacier passes and ascend important peaks with much less trouble than he can visit such an out-of-the-way place as Estes Park and climb the mountains which surround it. Many are undoubtedly familiar with the view of the Matterhorn as seen from Zermatt. The east face — the one seen from Zermatt — is generally spoken of as a precipice, and looks like one too; but Whymper said of it, in his

* It seems to me that the explanation of the formation of this cliff is not easily found; but I would refer others who, like myself, may have an interest in the question of the general formation of the range, to Clarence King's "Report of the Geological Exploration of the Fortieth Parallel," article "Colorado Range," Section I., by Arnold Hague.

account of his seventh attempt to climb the mountain, " that the east face was a gross imposition; it looked not far from perpendicular, while its angle was, in fact, scarcely more than 40°." The ascent of the Matterhorn from Breuil is probably one of the most difficult climbs that has ever been attempted and accomplished; yet when standing above Breuil, one can see plainly how the mountain is broken up into ledges, and in no place is there a vertical surface of more than 500 feet. A peak of peerless beauty in the Alps is the Zinal-Rothhorn, near Zermatt. Placed far back on the range, this mountain is not at all popular, and is not even visible from Zermatt, the great mountaineering centre. But those who have looked upon its steep sides from a near view-point would say that they had looked upon a precipice, and one who has scaled its cliffs would certainly carry away a vivid impression of the vertical. Although made up of a series of precipitous ledges, the mountain-side falls far short of making straight up and down lines. The opposite side of the Rothhorn also makes a grand rock-slope, too steep for snow to lie on, yet that is also placed at an angle of about 40°. But the tower on Long's Peak exposes an unbroken front of 1,200 feet, as smooth as the side of Bunker Hill Monu-

ment. Former estimates have credited the precipice with 3,000 feet of altitude. We should have
to look to the walls about the Yosemite, to find

The Cliffs of Long from the East Side.

anything superior in actual vertical heights to
those of the Front Range. I know that our party
lingered long gazing at this sheer cliff; and only

the fact that we were liable to be benighted in the forest forced us to hurry away.

We reached the limits of the " Bowlder Field " at 3.30 P. M., and mounting our horses were at Lamb's at 5.20 o'clock.   But, sad to relate, as we reached the lower edges of timber-line, we heard thunder booming on Estes Cone and saw flashes of lightning on the upper peaks.   The dashing rain was immediately upon us, and we rode into Lamb's enclosure at a gallop, camera and sensitized plates dancing on my horse's back at great risk, and all of us drenched by the torrents which were poured upon us.

II.

HIGH up on the northeastern slopes of Long's Peak is a lonely lake situated under the remarkable precipice.   Not easy of access, I was unable to visit it in 1887, but put this trip down in a list of expeditions for 1888.   Lamb wrote me during the winter reminding me that this alone was worth another trip to Estes Park, especially as no one, to his knowledge, had ever been beyond the lake to the base of the perpendicular cliff.

For the purpose of accomplishing this long-

contemplated trip, accompanied by my wife I
drove in a buckboard from Ferguson's to Lamb's

Lake on Long's Peak, Lily Mountain in the Distance.

early in the morning of July 11. The valley in
which Lamb's cabin is located lies between Lily
Mountain on the east and Long's Peak on the

west. Finding that we had the time for it, Carlyle Lamb and I ascended Lily Mountain in the
afternoon. We started for a point midway between the north and south peaks. These peaks
I have already referred to, as being called on the
plains the "Twin Sisters." In the ascent we
found a cold spring immediately under the final
ledges of the south peak. Lamb informs me that
good springs burst out from the ledges all along
the west side of the mountains. It hardly seems
as if enough snow and rain fell on the range to
keep up the supply, but the springs are ever-
flowing.

At four o'clock, two hours from the ranch, we
were on the summit of the north peak. The
clouds were high in the west, and at times obscured the sun, and their great shadows were seen
moving over the wide plain. The view of Long's
Peak was very fine, for, on account of our great
altitude (11,453 feet) and our proximity, we could
look into the upper cañons and gorges. The
tramp up Lily Mountain well repaid me, for it
yielded good results in photographs of the Front
Range from a new stand-point.

A friend joined us at Lamb's in the evening,
and early in the morning, accompanied by Carlyle,
we rode away, bound for the marvellous lake. We

followed the usual trail to the peak, to a point about 500 feet above timber-line, then bore off to the left, and, without ascending very much, reached the edge of the gorge which holds the tarn to which we were going. From the brink of this gorge several other lakes were seen resting far below us. Making the horses fast to some big rocks, we "let down," as Lamb's phrase has it, into the gorge. Descending as little as possible, we made for the water, which was hidden from view by a great dike which holds it in. We reached our goal at ten o'clock, three hours and a quarter from Lamb's. We estimated the size of the lake at a quarter of a mile long and one fifth of a mile wide. We skirted above it on the north side, and a half-hour was consumed in going the length of it. The occupation was neither climbing nor walking; it was a continual jumping from slab to bowlder. There is no beach by the lake, — only a mass of big rocks on the north and west sides. The dike on the east is solid and smooth, while on the south side a nearly vertical cliff runs down straight into the water to a great depth. Wherever there is a break in this cliff, snow fills the gullies, hangs over, and is mirrored in the water. There is no passage-way along that side. When we saw it the lake was free

4

from ice, with the exception of two small floating masses. The elevation is 11,000 feet.

We did not stop long at the lake, but continued on and up till we  reached the base of the snow-field, only the upper edges of which are visible from any point below or from any distant mountains that I had ascended. We followed the winding ice-stream

Winding Snow-field on Long's Peak.

for three quarters of an hour, and were greatly surprised to find a snow-field whose whole length it would surely require an hour for a fast walker to surmount from base to summit. In its winding course downward, the track of the snow-slope is first directly south, then turns east. Curving again sharply toward the north, a very steep arm joins it in the bend from the south. Soon it turns to the east, and is joined by another tributary from the north. The end of the trunk is about two hundred feet above the lake. The surface of the snow was hard and granular, and gave good footing, and ascending by it was much easier than by the rocks. At the base of the precipice the barometer registered 900 feet above the lake, making the elevation 11,900 feet, or 2,371 feet below the summit of the peak. This fact, together with other observations, gave us opportunity to estimate the height of the vertical cliff above us. Commencing 300 feet below the summit, the cliff plunges straight down for at least 1,200 feet, and is only a little removed from vertical for the remaining distance of nearly 900 feet. A stone thrown from the upper edge of the precipice, if projected out but a little, would reach the snow 2,000 feet below, before finding lodgment. While we were there, debris dislodged from a point half-way up fell upon the ice with a crash. We did not linger to investigate.

At a point on the snow which we paced off as

two hundred feet wide, we placed a number of cairns, in line with two larger stone men, — one placed on the lower or moraine side, and one on the ledges or upper side, — planning a second visit in order to observe whether the ice moved at all down the mountain. There was hardly any slope at this station. We observed but one crevasse, — a small one, about a foot wide, near the precipice. Against the base of the cliff and from the sides of the mountain the ice had pulled away, and deep chasms and rifts were shown.

Again, on July 28, we visited Lamb's ranch. This time Mr. Benjamin Ives Gilman was to be my companion in a second visit to the lake, snow-field, and precipice. An evening spent before Lamb's big fireplace is always enjoyable, and that night we discussed the probabilities of our meeting with some mountain lions that had been observed near the trail the day before.

In the morning we were ready to start at 6.40 o'clock. Close examination of our fire-arms made us shiver. I carried an old double-barrelled shot-gun, and was provided with a number of charges of buckshot; but one trouble with the weapon was that, after firing it, it was necessary to use a knife blade to press back the pins that discharged the cap. This would necessitate lively work in a

close encounter with a puma, if two shots did not
kill. Lamb gave Mr. Gilman his little revolver
with only three cartridges in it, which was all the
stock at the ranch. He reserved for himself a
small jack-knife. But notwithstanding our weak
armor we turned off from our route to the lake
when a little above timber-line at half-past eight,
and scrambled for an hour among the ledges where
the "lions" had been seen; but careful search
failed to reveal them, and we reasoned that they
had left the mountains, as there were no fresh
tracks. These beasts are very shy. Carlyle said
that one crossed his claim near the corral the
previous winter, but was never seen again; and
that he probably "lit out" of the valley on dis-
covering that it was inhabited by man.

Our going out of the way was repaid by the
glorious view that we had of the Front Range
from the ledges; but it required haste to reach
the lake by noon, which we did, and later
lunched far up under the precipice.

We then examined the line of cairns which
were on the snow. The end cairns, which had
been placed on a level with the snow, were now
six feet above it, showing that the snow had sunk
that amount. Mr. Gilman sighted across the line.
He looked amused. "How did you get them so

straight ? If you wanted to prove motion, why
did you not place them in a curve ? " The fact
was settled; there was no motion in that ice-
stream, though Lamb and I thought his remarks
rather complimentary to the thoroughness of our
work.

Section of Snow-field on Long's Peak.

The great amount of settling of the snow-field
seemed strange to us, as there appeared to be but
little surface melting; but we noted one fact
which explained it in part at least. At a point
where the trend of the snow crosses the gorge, and
on the lower side, is a lateral moraine, the top of
which is some twenty feet above the ice at its
lowest mark. Upon the lower side of this mo-

raine, and about sixty feet below the top, a torrent bursts out of the rocks, which comes from under the snow of the opposite side, and has worked its channel through the debris. The stream was such a one as would come from a fire-department hose, without nozzle and half turned off. The water spurted up about a foot.

This day we spent more time about the lake, and lingered long on the dike at its exit end. Notwithstanding the grand scenery above us, one thing below received our marked attention, and that was a great lateral moraine, which, commencing but a little way below our position, ran for a long distance down into the valley, and revealed what must have been the might of the ancient glacier that carried the stones down to form it. Similar scenes are repeated on the peaks near Long's, and all tell the same story. All along the Front Range to the westward of Estes Park, snow clings as beautiful cornices, cutting the sky-line in the sierra notches; as broad shining expanses it lies in hollows at the head of the deep cañons; in the form of icebergs it floats in semi-frozen lakes; and as bands or winding ice-streams it fills grooves on the rock fronts of precipitous peaks. The hot sun and clear dry air of Colorado have nearly prevailed in the struggle against the rule of ice, and what perpetual snows remain are but slight traces of the vast ice-fields that once covered the country. The creaking of grounded icebergs, the cracking of granulated snow, or the rumbling of waters under the rocks are but feeble mutterings in this nearly hushed and silent region of cliff and bowlder, compared with the crash of avalanche and roar of torrents that once must have reverberated among the crags and ledges.

In many parts of our continent, where rains have come in floods and all aerial forces have had full play, the tracing of past glacial action is only possible to the skilled and persevering geologist. In Colorado, however, on account of the lack of moisture and frost, many records of geological interest remain essentially unchanged by time, and we see uplifted strata near the mountain tops, banded structures of granite on the mountain sides, and morainal debris at the mountain base, the rocks remaining much as they were originally reared, compressed, or distributed. Age upon age of geologic time has passed since the ice crowded down the whole length of the gorges, and filled the narrow valleys, but the length and magnitude of the ancient glaciers are attested by the present aspect of these valleys; and though the active forces are confined to the mountain tops, their past work in the lower country is plainly seen, — more plainly, perhaps, than in any other locality. A series of mighty rocky barriers crosses the cañon beds at frequent intervals, marking the successive stages of the retreat of the ice up through the gorges; while, sweeping away from the base of the peaks, are great lateral moraines, many hundred feet high, extending to a considerable distance. Such is the huge moraine in Willow Park. Five hundred feet in height at the base of the mountains, it runs with true tapering lines far down into Estes Park, its limits being marked by a row of straggling bowlders. The path of the ancient glacier which brought down the rocks from the mountain tops to form the ridge, has been traced high up into the range, showing that it must have been at least ten miles long, with tributaries nearly as large.

On the opposite side of Long's Peak from that which we were exploring are a number of moraines similar in appearance to the one in Willow Park, but this one that we looked upon seemed to surpass them all in interest and in pictorial effect. It begins but a little way below the lake, and sweeps with a beautiful curve far down into the valley, looking like a great artificial embankment reared by a gigantic race of men. Differing from

the ledges of the foot-hills, and from the scarped
cliffs of the mountain flanks, this ridge is made
up of bowlders and debris ; and though over-
grown on its lower portions with spruce and pine,
its origin is evident to even those little versed in
glacial lore.   Few scenes in nature can be found
like this, where the observer can so easily throw
himself back into

The Great Moraine east of Long's Peak.

the geologic past.   Far above is the remnant of
the glacier, with its steep incline ; and though
our investigation proved it lacking in motion, yet
with its fields of *névé* and tributary couloirs it is
very glacial in appearance.   Spires of rock and
splintered crag tower above.   The wild amphitheatre of cliffs around has been swept of debris,

Across the Gorge to Escarpment of the East Peak.

and the place of deposit of the torn fragments lies far below ; for in the days of old, rocks that crumbled fell upon the moving ice-stream, which in its passage scooped out the lake bed and landed its freight in the valley.

In the distance, overlooking a beautiful valley, and past the wooded slopes of Lily Mountain, one sees the wide stretch of hazy plain, in appearance like the ocean in a calm, and can imagine himself back in the paleozoic age, when the great inland sea rolled to the westward before the mountains were uplifted and the waters retreated toward the gulf.

Surely, in resting on this dike, one dreams of a past and thinks not of the future. In descending from it this day we followed down the gorge farther than in the previous trip, in order to see some very pretty falls that tumbled over the ledges. At one point the height of the fall is seventy feet, while a little farther down stream is a second fall of a hundred feet. Standing below it the view is remarkable, for the great walls of Long's Peak are in the background.

This records my last expedition of importance on Long's Peak, and I would not fail to impress on the mind of the tourist that the scenes are too grand for words to convey a true idea of their magnificence. Let him, then, not fail to visit them.

III.

INTERESTING as the ascent of Long's Peak may be, no one expedition by any means exhausts the attractions of the mountain. Both upon its sides and at its base, removed from the beaten trails, are forests, glens, and brooks deserving of detailed exploration.

On July 4 I set out from Lamb's ranch, accompanied by Carlyle, in search of the homes of the beaver. We explored several streams to the south of the ranch in vain for new dams and occupied houses; but equipped as we were with a camera, we found plenty of amusement in investigating and photographing the ancient beaver works. On Rock Creek, which flows from the snows of Long's Peak, there are many of great interest. In the meadow through which this stream runs, an area of many acres is grown up with willows and intersected with a perfect network of old dams. The stream has been turned from its channel so many times that it zigzags in every direction. As a rule the novice would probably not detect the fact that these embankments are the work of beavers, for they are all turfed over and may be a century old. Some of them cross the meadows like causeways, others are covered with tall rich grass; but in one place we succeeded in getting an illustration which shows plainly the origin of the artificial ramparts. The stream had broken through the old dam, and had left exposed to view the manner of its construction. In places the earth had been washed away, leaving sticks projecting both parallel and

Old Beaver Dam.

at right angles to the length of the work. The sticks and twigs were well preserved. At places on the side of the embankment these sticks and mud were solid as if stratified in alternate layers. Near this broken dam we found the skull of a buffalo.

The old houses were very interesting; many appeared like heaps of branches and decayed wood. We discovered one, however, that was much more regular in its form than the new houses observed in other localities. The channel of the stream had been changed some yards from the house, trees and shrubs had fallen away, and the ancient dwelling, left on a high and dry spot, had settled into a regular conical heap. My observations in general lead me to think that the bea-

Old Beaver House.

vers do not intend to build their houses so as to be conspicuous, as often portrayed, but rather choose to have them appear as a mere heap of brush which might have collected in a natural manner.

Another day Mr. Hallett, Mr. Gilman, and I were exploring the sources of Wind River, upon the northern slopes of Long's Peak. Within a few years Mr. Sprague, the proprietor of the ranch in Willow Park, has cut a

New Beaver Dam.

trail to the peak, which runs by the side of this little stream for a few miles. At a point where it was a little too deep to ford, he laid down a few aspen-trees to answer for a bridge. Our route intersected this trail, and we made use of it for some distance; but when we came to the banks of the stream, we found its passage impossible, for a large deep pool lay immediately in the place where the trail led down to the brook. For a moment the cause of the pool was a mystery, but peering beyond we caught a glimpse of the newly made dam, and there dawned upon us the explanation of the disappearance of the lightly built bridge. To save labor the cunning beavers had made use of the cut aspens, and had worked the greater part of them into their dam. It took us over an hour to cut an opening through the woods at a place where we found a suitable ford to cross the stream, and thus flank the breastworks of the obstructionists.

After quite a long search we discovered the recently built house, hidden among aspens and willows in such a wild spot that, without having seen the breakwater in the stream below, no one would have suspected the existence of the dwelling. Clear cool water flowed by its base. Mirrored in the pool one would hardly know where the trees and tangled brush ended. The house was placed on the edge of the stream, and some of the poles forming it projected over the water, so that the

edifice seemed to overhang. A well-worn path
led from a steep bank near the log and mud house
up through the forest. Large trees lately felled
lay around, and had been completely stripped of
their bark. From the freshly cut twigs observed,
it was evident that the animals had been at work
the night previous, and only a few hours before
our arrival. Under a tree we found a number of

Inhabited Beaver House.

freshly cut sticks, all of the same length, — about
eighteen inches, — and of a nearly uniform diameter, — one and one-half inches, — which we sup-
posed the beavers had provided to use for dividing
the interior of their house into apartments, or
more probably to make an upper room. This
latter work they accomplish by thrusting one end

"We three."

of the sticks into the sides of the house from the inside, the other end projecting nearly to the centre of the interior. Placed thus in a circle, an opening is left through which the animal can crawl and rest high and dry. This upper story is necessary, because the streams are liable to rise suddenly and flood the ground floor.

Dependent principally upon aspens and willows for food, the beaver is certainly hard pressed now to maintain his " claims " in Estes Park, for the pre-empters are fast taking up all the land where these trees thrive. Higher up in the cañons, the willows entirely disappear, the aspens are scarce, and there will soon be nothing for the beaver to do but to migrate beyond the range.

This day we spent so much time among the beaver works that the object of the expedition, an intended trip to the headquarters of the south fork of the Thompson, was defeated; but a pro-spective hard tramp was replaced by an enjoyable scramble in the afternoon among ledges on the slopes of Long's Peak; and this, with the episode of the beaver dam and the bagging of grouse, that fell to our gun, made the day one of the most delightful that I passed in the Rockies.

PRECIPICE ON MOUNT HALLETT.

CHAPTER III.

A FTER having made the ascent of Long's Peak and a number of lower elevations, I was bent on investigating the rock walls of the range that extend around to the northwest from Long's Peak to Hague's Peak, the eastern face of which in many places rivals the mural cliff of Long's Peak itself. As observed from high points in the centre of Estes Park, it is evident that there is but one pass in the chain, and that is over Table Mountain. The rest of the range is one solid rampart, — at least as far as Willow Cañon, — and impassable for pack mules.

In the northern Rockies the difficulties to be considered when attempting to cross the chain depend upon whether pack-mules and horses can be gotten over it or not; for it must be remembered that their aid is absolutely necessary for the success of any long expedition, as there is no comfortable hotel, nor even a log-cabin, to be found on the western side of the ridge. For hunting expeditions the beasts have to carry blankets, flour, coffee or tea, salt, and pork; no sugar or milk is allowed. For such an expedition as is to be described, a pack animal is not generally required; but as I had a camera and plates to carry, it was necessary for me to have a horse, and to ride as far as possible. The ideal way to climb mountains is to have nothing whatever to carry, — no camera, no theodolite, no rifle, — nothing to load one down, except perhaps a cracker and a bottle of cold tea to sustain one's self during the walk. But in all my ventures during the summer of 1887 I carried my photographic apparatus to the highest ledges. Therefore I always rode a horse as far above timber-line as a route could be found for him.

The first difficulty which presents itself to the mountaineer in Colorado is a lack of guides; there is much trouble about securing them to accompany one even as far as trails go and as far as a horse can carry. The hunters object to climbing or walking; and although very familiar with the country, hunting as they do all around the peaks, it is rarely that they climb to the mountain tops. One of their number, a dweller in an upper park, told me that he did not "see anything in the high mountains, and did not know about the scenery."

"Yes," said a listener, "he don't know about anything but ' bar.' "

But our little company at Ferguson's was well provided with a leader in the person of a gentleman who has a cottage near this ranch, who spends all the summer months in the mountains and knows thoroughly every trail and stream for many miles around. To him I am indebted for all that I saw of the Front Range, excepting in my ascent of Long's Peak and of some of the lower elevations.

Peak of Mount Hallett.

The sharpest peak in the Front Range, as seen from the valley of the Big Thompson Creek,

which runs through Estes Park, is a mountain
near the centre of the range, to the left of Table
Mountain. It rises from the large snow-field
which hangs like a true glacier to a steep ridge
connecting the peak with Table Mountain. For
several weeks I had looked with longing eyes at
this peak and its snow surroundings, wishing to
climb it in a single day from Ferguson's ranch,
and to do this in connection with a ride over
Table Mountain toward Middle Park. When our
acknowledged leader proposed taking our little
company, consisting of a member of the Appalachian Mountain Club, the surgeon, and myself,
over the mill trail to the continental divide, I had
no doubt that my plans would succeed.

The day fixed upon was late in August. We
were to have been off at six o'clock, but it was
half past six before we left the ranch. We intended to take a barometer, but our leader dropped
it on the porch as we were packing, and it *fell*
three thousand feet. We rode off, however, in
good spirits, thinking ourselves fortunate in getting started even so early, for the horses had to be
" rounded up " for us ; and Tom, the mule, galloped
all over the hillside before he was captured.

We rode down the hill and crossed the Big
Thompson Creek, recrossed it to the Wind River

Valley, then over the Wind River and south branch of the Thompson, and followed the latter by a road leading through sage-brush until we came to a flat meadow and ranch at the base of the mountain.

We reached this ranch at about eight o'clock, then followed the rapid stream up through tall aspens to an old saw-mill. The timber is very heavy on this mountain, but the mill did not pay financially, as the lumber had to be hauled so far to market; so everything has been abandoned and has gone to ruin. We were now by the side of Timber Creek, and in twenty minutes struck the trail leading through tall spruce, and left all sound of tinkling cow-bells and lowing of cattle far below us. The wood was dark, the ground damp, and wonderful flowers and moss grew on the trail. Deep-colored Painted Cups, and the tiny fragrant bells of the *Linnæa borealis,* the white *Pyrola chlorantha,* the curious Lousewort (*Pedicularis racemosa*), and the *Arnica alpina* gleamed out of this green darkness. These flowers were carefully transferred to boxes, for the inspection of botanists down at Ferguson's, to whom also we carried several genuine alpine plants, found far up toward the mountain tops.

We found a deep snow-bank in among the trees

a little below timber-line, which is at about eleven thousand feet above sea-level on this, the north-eastern side of the range. Here we turned off from the trail to a ledge a few steps away, from which we had a wonderful view, through a deep gorge, of the rocks belonging to the peak which we intended to scale. A thousand feet below us was a large lake, which appeared dark as night and is evidently very deep, as the sides run down steep from the edges; we called it " Black Lake." A little higher up was another, from which the eye followed up the ravine, over bowlder waste and white snow coverings, to the large snow-field, which looked still more like a glacier than it did from the valley below. It is evident from the succession of moraines that a mighty ice-stream once filled the entire length of the cañon.

This scene, which has been looked upon by very few persons, is certainly alpine. Taken in con-junction with the view of the tower of Long's Peak rising in the southeast three thousand feet above the observer and exposing a grand slope with a lake nestling at its feet, few sublimer sights can be met with in the chain of the Rockies.*

From the opposite side of the gorge, a vertical

* See Frontispiece.

wall rises to a height of not less than one thousand feet; the face of it nearly perpendicular, —
a marvellous exhibition on a stupendous scale of
the geological phenomenon of cleavage.   The surface of the ridge that we stood upon is broken
in masses, bowlders, and blocks, — a wilderness of
debris unevenly distributed, while upon the precipice there are no signs of uneven demolition or
aqueous erosion.   The rocks cleave off evenly in
straight up and down planes along the whole
extent of the face.

After leaving the timber the trail is very in-
distinct, — indeed there can hardly be said to be
any trail at all, a possible way for horses being
marked merely by stones placed one upon another
at long intervals.   These were set there by our
leader or some hunter, on a previous trip.

While among these rocks we shot a ptarmigan.
The first warning we received of the proximity
of this bird was seeing the half-grown young,
about the size of quail, running around or taking
flight to a distance; they were evidently able to
take care of themselves.   Then we discovered the
old bird crouching on a rock, its wings spread out
so as to lie as flat as possible, and showing a
few white feathers on them.   This bird is heavy,
though not quite so large as the grouse, but its

power of flight is wonderful. When frightened it will rise immediately and shoot over the top of a high peak, far away. This one was only waiting for all its young to disappear by flight or hiding, before it would fly towards the western mountains. Later in the season the ptarmigan is perfectly white, approaching this condition gradually. In winter the feet are covered with white downy feathers, while in summer they are nearly bare. When disturbed in the winter they fly to the snow-fields, where it is almost impossible to distinguish their white forms.

An old moraine among the rocks near where we saw the ptarmigan, was distinctly traceable for several hundred feet down the mountain, by rounded stones piled in a curving row about two feet high, reminding one of a stone-wall in the Berkshire hills.

A little farther on in the ascent we had a great surprise. We were keeping very quiet and were on the lookout for ptarmigan, when we came upon three Rocky Mountain sheep, quietly browsing only a few hundred feet distant on our right. Our leader told us to duck, and said in an undertone to me, " Follow me with your camera." I did so, and all of us dismounted and almost crawling along soon saw the big-horn again, though

they had not observed us. The wind was blowing
a gale in our faces, so they had no scent of us.
Luckily my instrument was focussed. I pointed
the lens at the animals and exposed one plate,
although they were not so near to us as when we
first saw them. They now discovered us, and
after a glance in our direction trotted off over the
slope to the brow of the hill. It was remarkable
how easily they moved over rocks and bowlders
among which we could hardly find a way for our
horses and mule. Imagine our surprise when
they turned and walked a little way towards us
again. I asked my friends to return to the packs
for more plates, and while they were gone I
focussed more carefully on the still distant animals, as they stared at me, their curiosity over-
coming their fear. My companions now brought
up the relay of fresh plates, and retired behind
some ledges farther off. At this moment, as I
remained there alone by the camera, the ram stood
up on his hind legs and struck out with his fore-
feet as if inviting combat; then the three stood
looking at me. We were in one of the wildest
spots on the mountains; a seemingly endless
field of ledge and bowlder all around, snow mountains and rocky peaks only in the panorama; all
signs of valley or glen, tree or river, far below.

I had a moment to reflect on what I was beholding, and carefully adjusting the glass again on
these rare creatures, closely watched them.

Our leader crawled up towards me, and as the
quarry showed signs of alarm I attempted to take
another picture; but I was now so excited that I
took a slide out of one plate-holder before putting
the cap on, and that ruined piece of glass now lies
among the rocks to amuse the conies and ptarmigan, while the slide which I had placed on the
camera was whirled far away by the strong wind.
Even so experienced a hunter as my companion
lost his head as the big-horn were trotting away,
and exclaimed, "Take them quick, take them
quick!" Then, as they stopped once more and
looked at us, he called himself bad names, saying,
"I might have known they would stop again, and
that there was no need of haste." But lo! what
did these sheep do but turn around and walk de-
liberately toward us until they were within about
a hundred feet! We were fairly trembling with
excitement, and I first took off the cap without
pulling the slide. When I made this blunder
they were all facing us, standing on granite ped-
estals a little elevated above the general level, and
in line with the broad snow-field on the cliffs
back of them, which showed them in relief with

The Quarry.

startling clearness. But the one seen in the background in the illustration then turned ; the others stepped down from their bold positions, and the best opportunity was lost. The next moment I succeeded in capturing them as seen in the picture; and then the animals decided to trot off, and we saw them no more.

Hunters talk of the excitement which a novice experiences when he shoots at his first buck, but I could have shot those three big-horn without being one half so nervous as when trying to photograph them.

Of the five plates which I used in trying to capture the big-horn on glass, three proved worthless besides the light-struck one already referred to, and it was indeed exceptional good fortune that I was enabled to secure even one picture of these very shy animals. When one reflects that hunters are obliged to use every precaution in approaching their haunts, and sometimes are obliged to lie concealed for hours, or to crawl on the edge of dizzy precipices in order to obtain a distant shot, he will realize the value of what we saw and took away with us. I certainly wish the noble ram and his little company a long and happy life among the wild crags of the great Front Range; and may the rifleman's bullet never bring low the beautiful pair of horns carried so grandly by the leader of the quarry!

This shy, beautiful creature is fast disappearing even from the wild mountain tops, and soon traces of him may be as rare as of his former pursuer, the Indian, of whom but one not very lasting mark remains in the valley of the Big Thompson Creek.

The photograph of the big-horn naturally occupies the place of honor among a great many pictures which I took in the Rockies, most of which were secured from very high elevations. The reader will perhaps pardon a little boasting when he realizes that such luck has probably never befallen a mountaineering photographer before. European climbers have been photographing for years in the high Alps, and even in more remote regions, but I doubt if a chamois has ever sat for his likeness, for it is rarely that one is closely approached. When I gaze at my picture of the big-horn and recall their appearance on the wild apex of our continent, I think of Tyndall's description of a day on the Great Aletsch Glacier, in which he tells of watching the approach of a chamois, till through his field glass he "could see the glistening of its eyes," but "soon it made a final pause, assured itself of its error [in approaching so near], and flew with the speed of the wind to its refuge in the mountains." Even by early travellers, the mountain sheep is described as very shy and difficult of approach. Fremont's description of his first sight of this animal is very interesting: —

" It was on the 12th of June, 1843, that we first saw this remarkable animal. We were near the confluence of the Yellowstone River with the Missouri, when a group of them, numbering twenty-two in all, came in sight. This flock was composed of rams and ewes, with only one young one or lamb among them. They scampered up and down the hills, much in the manner of common sheep; but notwithstanding all our anxious efforts to get within gun-shot, we were unable to do so, and were obliged to content ourselves with the first sight of the Rocky Mountain ram." *

Persons who are unfamiliar with the game in the Rockies, or who have no idea of the wildness of the big-horn, I would refer to the pages of that very interesting book by Baillie-Grohman, " Camps in the Rockies," or to a paper by W. S. Rainsford in " Scribner's Magazine " for September, 1887; and after reading either or both of these accounts of the chase of the big-horn, I think they will agree that it was a marvel that

* Quadrupeds of North America, J. J. Audubon, edition of 1854, vol. ii. p. 166.

such an animal could ever be photographed among the wild crags of his native ranges.

Very soon after the adventure with the big-horn we reached the top of Table Mountain. The outlook was grand on all sides. We were out of the bowlder field, and could almost gallop our horses in any direction on the pebbly surface. We

View from Table Mountain Southward.

rode to the west end of the mountain, which we reached at one o'clock, and looked right down upon the glacier-furrowed Middle Park, and upon Grand Lake, the large sheet of water in it. This side of the mountain was broken up into ledges, not very abrupt however. The distant lines of snowy ranges were very sharp and clear in the west, and the mountains of the Front Range around us somehow seemed higher above us than they did from the valley below. We rode back towards the peak to some water, where there was feed for the horses, and ate our lunch; but the surgeon and I made quick work of that, and left at quarter before two for our new peak, the real goal of my eyes. We rode up the western slope, which was a very gradual ascent, to the highest patch of grass, and were surprised to find how far up we had been able to ride. We then tethered the animals, and at quarter past two attacked the rocks. We could have found a more gradual but longer ascent by bearing around to the right and keeping more to the southern side; but for the interest of the ridge, and that we might have the snow and deep gorge in view, we bore to the left, up the edge, and after a short and rather easy climb reached the summit. The peak looks quite steep, but is deceptive. It is made up of a heap of rocks, and no ledges or precipices are upon any side but the north and northeast. We found a cairn on the summit, which was probably piled up years ago by some indefatigable member of the Survey party. Among the many peaks climbed in the West I found but three that I had any reason to believe had not been ascended before.

We stayed on the summit for half an hour, and studied the landscape. The view is not as extended as from Long's Peak, though nearly as fine. The great mass of Mummy Mountain, higher than our peak, hid North Park and much of the Medicine Bow Range in the northwest; but the view of Middle Park was much finer than from Long's Peak, as we were right over it. Grand Lake lay just below us. We could trace the course of the river which it feeds, winding through the deep valley on its way towards the great Colorado River and the Pacific Ocean, while on the northeast we could follow the mountain torrents that run into the Platte, and find their way to the Gulf of Mexico to be tossed about at last in the Atlantic.

The area of the summit was very limited, and a good view in every direction was obtained from any rock. Lightning had evidently lately struck on the top of the peak, for freshly broken slabs were strewn around.

We scanned the depths of the gorges below, and all the rock-strewn waste of Table Mountain, hoping to have one more glimpse of the big-horn, but they had gone to the more distant range. A wilder scene than we looked upon, they cannot find, nor better hiding-places, nor a more awful series of cliffs to wander among than the ravines of Mount Hallett.

We ran down the peak faster than we went up, keeping yet nearer to the precipice ; and when we came to the head of the snow bank, we walked out upon it, kicking in steps with our heels, until it ran off so steep that it would have been dangerous to have ventured farther without ice-axe and ropes. There were no actual crevasses, but the snow was ridged and serrated. The centre of the field seemed to be solid ice, and there was a miniature *bergschrund* next the upper rocks bordering on the ice.

Time pressed, for we had crowded much work into one day ; so we hurried on, and mounting our horses, gained our friends near the opposite side of the snow. We had more trouble in finding a way down through the bowlders than in going up, but we finally sighted the trail at timber-line, emerged from the woods into the flat country at eight o'clock, and, with some " throwing in of steel," reached Ferguson's at nine o'clock.

VIEW DOWN THE GORGE BETWEEN TABLE AND HALLETT MOUNTAINS.

CHAPTER IV.

A YEAR'S absence from the glorious Rockies only tended to strengthen my interest in many scenes among them. Not the least important of these was the great snow-field lying in the gorge between Table Mountain and Mount Hallett, and referred to in the chapter devoted to the last-named mountain. On July 3, 1888, I was able to visit it for the purpose of making measurements to ascertain whether there might not be some appreciable motion in a body of snow of such magnitude. This and subsequent expeditions involved much hard work, though of a pleasurable nature. The results were far from satisfactory; they will be presented here, however, for what they are worth, for the benefit of any future observers who may chance to read this book.

I had been preparing for the trip for several days, and had sharpened a number of stakes to drive into the ice, so that on visiting the spot again in August it could readily be determined whether given masses of ice had moved down the slope. Unable to find any one at Ferguson's who cared to undergo the fatigue of the ascent, I asked Carlyle Lamb to join me. He kindly consented, and not only proved exceedingly obliging and helpful, but also a very agreeable companion. He rode over to our ranch at six o'clock, and we were off at seven. Lamb carried the bundle of stakes and my sensitized plates on his horse, leaving me only the tripod and small traps to bother with. He had never been over the trail before, and I only once ; but there was no trouble in finding the narrow path through the forest, which we reached in an hour.

Twelve o'clock found us on the top of Table Mountain,* and tethering the horses we shouldered our packs and descended the gorge to the base of the ice, a thousand feet below. We did considerable exploring before selecting our route, and then found that we had taken the hardest one conceivable, for we were immediately landed in a maze of tremendous bowlders, and it took us an hour to reach the lower edge of the snow. At one point, when paying particular attention to my

* Barometric observations this day gave the height of the nearly vertical cliffs of Mount Hallett as 1,100 feet.

footing, a strong gust of wind took off my hat,
carried it over a high ridge and dropped it down
in another cañon; so I was without headgear for
the rest of the day.

The snow-field fills an amphitheatre, over a
quarter of a mile in width at the lower rim, with
walls a thousand feet high. The general slope is
northeast. The position in width is northwest to
southeast. A magnificent terminal moraine locks
in the ice, and the meltings from the snow escape
under the rocks of the moraine at least fifty feet
below the top. The subterranean waters roared
on all sides. Such a wilderness of bowlders I had
never been in before. All the rocks composing
the moraine have come from the cliffs above,
which now show but a narrow line above the ice,
except on the left, or Mount Hallett, side; this
mountain still contributes bowlders and debris to
the ice below. On the right side a few hundred
feet of cliffs still remain, and enormous blocks had
recently fallen on the ice. The greater part of
the moraine was undoubtedly formed when the
body of the snow was much greater than it is
now, not in area, but in depth; yet I think the
work of carrying down stones is still going on.
At the base, on the right side, the field is divided,
and the ice extends farther down than it does in

the centre. From this division a great medial moraine begins, which rivals the terminal in size, and extends a long way down the gorge.

I selected the upper edge of this medial moraine for my first stake, and crowding it into the dirt, braced it up with small stones. Lamb then went out on the ice and set the stakes at intervals, in line with a rock on the Mount Hallett side of the gorge, I giving him directions as to positions with a wave of the hand. Thus he placed eight sticks in the ice. The opposite side was very steep, and he experienced much trouble in ascending it ; if the snow had not been rough, he could not have accomplished the work. In the centre, where stakes Nos. 3, 4, and 5 were set, it was slippery, and the snow had been compressed into solid ice. After the line was completed I photographed the range, the end of the moraine with stake No. 1 for the foreground, and the opposite rock in the centre of the distant view.

I then went along the line as far as No. 5, and with a hatchet hammered the posts in firmly. We measured the distance from No. 4 to the terminal moraine, where we made a cairn and found it 162 feet. Having some stakes left, we placed one seventy feet higher up the slope than No. 4, and two more above, at distances apart of thirty-five feet ; so that the highest one was in the centre of the ice-field, and 302 feet above the moraine. In order to place these stakes we were obliged to chop holes in the ice, fill in around the stakes and stamp around them, as if setting fence-posts in earth. It took us two hours to accomplish this task, and it was three o'clock before we were ready to climb up the ledges. Several routes being open to our inspection, a much easier one was found than we had used in the descent.

Again on Monday, July 16, I went up a little above timber-line on Table Mountain. From a ledge that I reached I observed that the extent of the glare ice in the centre of the snow-field had increased. The weather had been very warm, and had evidently consolidated much of the snow.

On July 25, with Mr. Gilman I started for a third visit to Table Mountain, to look after the set stakes. We carried with us two ropes, respectively twenty-three and thirty-two feet long, for the purpose of measurement. Leaving Ferguson's at six o'clock A. M., we made rapid progress, till when near the summit. Here, owing to my bad guiding, we took a course too low down on the north slopes of the mountain. Among some rough bowlders one of the horses fell and delayed us for half an hour. The animal's legs were caught in such a manner that he seemed only able to flounder. We endeavored to get him out with the aid of the ropes, but all help seemed to make matters worse, and we gave it up. We were a pair of sad and helpless mortals. We were already talking of killing him to prevent a lingering death, when the beast managed to extricate himself, and, though badly cut, as soon as we led him to a grassy spot he began to browse in company with his mate.

An hour after this adventure we were on the snow. All of the stakes were found down, and all my labor had been expended for naught, at least so far as reliable evidence goes. One fact, however, is perhaps worth recording. Stake No. 4 was twenty-four feet below the line. One of the stakes originally put above it had moved thirty-two feet, another twenty-eight feet, which would give an average of twenty-eight feet motion in twenty-two days, or $1\frac{6}{22}$ feet per day.* These three stakes were lying in little depressions, such

* Such great motion in so small an ice-field (amounting to its total length in three years) seems improbable. However, this series of stakes was placed in the centre of the expanse, and at a point where the flow of ice from the south, the west, and the east seemed to join, the figures may be approximately correct. As the weather had been very warm the condition of the snow may have been such as would be requisite for the maximum of motion.

as might have resulted from our chopping on the surface of the snow. The fourth stake in the series had moved fifty-two feet, but was lying on a flat surface; so this one is left out of the calculation. How much of this motion was due to sliding of the sticks or to a real flowing of ice must remain for future observation to determine. The stakes set on the steeper portions of the ice were found on the moraine.

The surface extent of the snow-field was about the same as when we first visited it, but it had sunk about six feet, — very little, I think, by surface wasting. There was a continual rush of water under the moraine, but very little water running in rills on the ice.

On regaining the horses I took off my flannel shirt, cut off the sleeves, and bound them around "Frank's" wounded legs. We had a dismal journey home, being obliged to lead our lame horse all the way. But the accident proved a great blessing to the animal. Exempted from all work for the balance of the season, he passed the happiest summer of his existence since he was a colt. To his evident delight he could safely nibble around close to the ranch without fear of being driven into the corral to be saddled for the use of the unfeeling tourist. In short, he became a guest of the

place, and boarded at the expense of my friend
and myself.

A week or two after this adventure Mr. Edmands, Professor Fay, Mr. Gilman, and I walked
from Ferguson's to the summit of Table Mountain
and back in a day. Though the wind on the top
was something furious, the two first-named gentle-

men made the ascent of Mount Hallett in addition. Under a sheltering ledge my companion
and I passed the intervening time watching cloud
effects on Long's Peak in the distance, or in looking down to the scene of our labor on the snow
below. The appearance of the ice was about the
same as when last visited. A few more crevasses
had opened high up on the northwest side. It

was interesting to compare this snow-field with others we had explored. It ranks third in size of those in the locality.

From what facts I have been able to glean from old residents in the valleys, the seasons of 1886, 1887, and 1888 seem to mark the period of minimum snow-fall. I am able to prove from photographs that there was less snow on the mountains in 1888 than in 1887. It would appear that much of the ice forming such large bodies as the mass in Table Mountain gorge must be quite old, as from reports there has not been snow-fall enough of late to make such an accumulation. I was at a loss to account for the great extent of this particular snow-field, till Mr. Hallett gave me a clew gained from his winter's residence in the mountains. It seems that Table Mountain, being flat-topped and having an immense area, is swept by the wind-storms of winter, and when other peaks are covered with snow, it is almost entirely bare. The snow is blown into the gorge, and there accumulates. While not nearly so picturesque as the winding glacier-like snows of Long's Peak, it is more interesting, as there must be three times as much ice in the gorge. The explanation of its size cannot be extended to account for that of the Hallett glacier, as there is no such flat-top mountain near by to feed it with snow; and to explain the size of this ice-field we must take into consideration its greater altitude, and perhaps allow a larger amount of precipitation of snow. It is undoubtedly true that there is more rain-fall on the Mummy Range and in Willow Cañon than there is on Table Mountain.

In descending Table Mountain this day, we followed the edge of the gorge nearly down to timber-line. The ledges overhanging the gorge on the Table Mountain side, not far from the summit, are truly grand, and recall the words of Burroughs: "There is a fascination about ledges. Time, old as the hills and older, looks out of their scarred and weather-worn faces. The woods are of to-day, but the ledges, in comparison, are of eternity."

Lower down the rocks are firmer, and resemble the cliffs on the Mount Hallett side. Yet instead of presenting a smooth front, short cañons run into the sides of the mountain. Very steep are the beds of these gorges, and little sheets of water lie far below. Everything here is on a grand scale, and it was with reluctance that we turned our backs on Table Mountain, perhaps for the last time.

THE HALLETT GLACIER.

CHAPTER V.

THE Mummy is an immense mountain in northern Colorado, lying directly north of Long's Peak and in line with the centre of Estes Park. It is a spur range running out to the eastward from a point where the Front Range, Rabbit Ear, and Medicine Bow Mountains nearly meet. It has its name from its fancied resemblance to an Egyptian mummy reclining at full length, and the range has been so called for some years. The highest point, Hague's Peak (13,832 feet, King), forms the head, and a height about two miles farther to the west marks the knees of the seeming prostrate figure.

On the north side of this west peak of Mummy Mountain is a large snow-field, of unusual interest on account of recent developments regarding its true character. It was discovered only a few years ago by a hunter named Israel Rowe, and in the following manner: It was in the time of the great grasshopper raid, when these insects

7

flew over the range from Utah to Colorado; myriads of them fell on the snow-fields in their passage, and many bears went up from the rocks to feed upon them. Hunters learning of this went up also to shoot the bears; and in such an expedition Rowe discovered what he called "the largest snow-field in the Rockies." Later he took two other hunters to see it. He afterward died while on a long hunt, but before his death mentioned this interesting discovery to the leader of our numerous expeditions in and about Estes Park. Four years ago Mr. Hallett visited it entirely alone, and nearly lost his life under circumstances which led him to wonder whether this snow-field might not be a glacier.

I had seen many snow-fields in the Rocky Mountains, but none where the body and weight of the snow were sufficient to form a true glacier; therefore, hearing Mr. Hallett's story, I was very anxious to have an opportunity to ascend the Mummy, and, relying on my knowledge gained in Alpine climbs, determine the nature of this one, — a desire which happily I was able to realize. At the time of my visit the great snow-field had probably never been seen by other than the persons above referred to, not only because so little had been said about it, but also on account of the distance and the difficulty of reaching it. The expedition requires parts of three days, and few travellers have the facilities for carrying provisions and blankets so far. Our leader, however, seeing that our ambition was unflagging, offered to show the possible glacier to another member of the Appalachian Mountain Club and myself; and so, on Monday, August 1, a folding mattress, blankets, provisions, axe, and coffee-pot — in short, a complete camping-outfit — were packed on Tom, the mule, and mounting our horses at 1 P. M., and leading Tom behind us, we rode away from Ferguson's Ranch toward the Black Cañon. I carried, strapped to the back of my saddle, a camera and tripod, and a package of sensitized dry plates. It had been my intention to take some stakes also, and to run a line of them across the snow-field for future observation, but I found that it was all that I could possibly do to carry my photographic apparatus to that altitude.

Our trail led up through the cañon, under enormous cliffs on the right, than which there are few finer, though on the left or south side the steep walls are lacking. Above the cañon the trail winds to the left, high above the brook, and runs between two mountains thickly clad with spruce. It is identical with the one leading to Lawn Lake.

From there on, however, there is no trail, and even to this point there was no sign of the path's having been traversed for a year. Our leader showed great skill in guiding us among bowlders and through tangled dwarf spruce over the ridge of Mummy Mountain to a good camping-place.

In crossing the ridge east of the Mummy's head, we had gone far above timber-line, but now had dropped down several hundred feet into the black spruce on the north side, in order to get firewood. This dwarf evergreen is very peculiar. The trees are not more than shoulder high, but the trunks, in many cases, are a foot or two in thickness. We found plenty of dead wood for our fire, and after unloading we picketed our animals in good feed and had our supper. This was chiefly from cold supplies, for we cooked nothing on the trip except coffee and toast. The altitude of our camp was about eleven thousand feet. The full moon shone brightly, and the night was very clear. We could see very easily the star ε Lyræ as double, much plainer indeed than I ever saw it as such at sea-level. Our big blazing fire must have been seen from the plains far away. As a general rule hunters in the West do not make large fires, contradicting in this respect the Indian saying that "white man make heap big fire, git way off;

Injun make little bit fire, stay close by." The
hunters do not sleep by a fire, but depend upon
blankets and canvas covers for warmth.

We turned in early, slept well, and were up
before the sun, that we might see it rise out of
the plains. And such a sunrise as we beheld !
The flat country of Larimer County is covered
with artificial lakes; and as the sun came up we
counted thirty-five small sheets of water glistening in its bright rays. The sky was clear, except
high in the east where a mass of clouds was gor-
geously colored. First picketing our animals in
a new place, we then had our own breakfast. We
had aimed to make an early start, but with all our
expeditiousness we did not get our animals saddled
and under us until seven o'clock.

We had considerable difficulty in getting
through the dwarf spruce, which was very thick.
The heavy snows of winter bow down the tops,
leaving them one mass of tangled branches and
twigs, while under the trees the footing for the
horses is very rough. However, in half an hour
we were out of the small timber, and riding over
a smooth grassy surface by the side of a deep
gorge on our right, which was surmounted by
steep cliffs and a large snow-field. The gorge was
a wild, desolate scene, it being the former pathway

of a glacier; down through it rocks were piled upon rocks for miles.

We reached the limits of the grass patches at nine o'clock, and could ride no farther. Leaving the horses, we walked up the rather steep ascent,

Ancient Bed of Hallett Glacier.

arriving at the foot of the snow-field in an hour. We had seen the upper snows for two hours, but had no view of the whole mass until we were right upon it; for an immense rocky ridge heaped high around the base hides three quarters of the snow-field until it is surmounted. All at once this scene burst upon us. A steep snow-bank extended about a thousand feet above to the top of the mountain. The water which had collected at its base had been frozen again,— not solidly, but with occasional open spaces in which large blocks of ice were floating around. As the force of the wind moved them, they were lifted up by rocks or firmer ice from beneath, creaking and groaning ; then broken up into fragments, but only to form new floes. The long line of the lower edge of the ice and snow curled over in beautiful combings as it hung over the open water.

The snow expanse is about a quarter of a mile in width, and entirely fills a kind of amphitheatre made by the main range of the Mummy and a spur which extends around to the northeast. In some places it makes the sky-line, but for the most part pointed rocks and towers jut up from the snow. One shaft, which we judged twenty feet in height, could not have been more than twelve inches in diameter at the base, and was of pure white quartz. The more easily decomposed granite had fallen away, leaving this firmer vein of rock standing alone. The whole extent of the snow was covered with grooves, markings, and cracks ; a large crevasse began near the south end and extended a long way into the centre, and close examination revealed many more above and below it, running parallel with it. The longest

of these was about a hundred feet above the water
at the southern extremity. Our leader said that
when he visited the place four years before there
were larger icebergs in the water. It is evident
how these were formed ; for when the large crevasses, near the water, are crowded toward the
lake, the masses of ice must fall off into it, repeat-

Ledges above the Hallett Glacier.

ing on a small scale what happens when the ice-
masses fall from the Humboldt Glacier into the
Arctic Ocean.

A single glance at the series of crevasses was
enough to convince me that we looked upon a
glacier, and further examination of the ice con-
firmed the first impression. The great ridge upon

which we stood was evidently a terminal moraine
formed by the glacier in past ages. What debris
comes down with the ice at the present time must
fall into the lake. The surface of the glacier,
however, is remarkably free from stones and
bowlders, caused, as we afterward determined, by
the fact that the loosened masses above the ice
fall to the west down the much steeper rock-fall
of the mountain ; yet at one point the ledges are
breaking away toward the glacier, and a few
bowlders are already embedded in the ice and are
on their way down the slide.

Having taken two pictures of the glacier and
lake from the moraine, accompanied by our leader,
I carried the camera back from the ice and took a
more distant view ; meanwhile the Appalachian
had strolled along to the south end to look at the
big crevasse. It seemed desirable to secure three
negatives of this section of the ice ; but as we had
only one sensitized plate with us, I started back
to the foot of the glacier, where we had left the
lunch and other luggage, for another plate-holder
containing two plates. And now an episode occurred which for the time being quite eclipsed
the pleasurable excitement of our discovery with
one of a more thrilling, if less agreeable sort. I
had gone about half-way when my companion

called out, " A bear ! a bear ! come here quick !"
I turned, ran back, and saw an immense range
grizzly standing on a rock about two hundred
feet from us; he had just come out from behind
a huge bowlder. I took his picture as quickly
as possible. This was probably the first time
that " old Ephraim" had ever had his picture

taken in his own
haunts; and if he
could only have
known what was
required of him,
he might just as
well have *sat* for
it. I then saw
the Appalachian,
standing very near to the bear, but back of him,
looking at him through his field-glass as coolly as
could be. The bear was of tremendous size, and
must have weighed a thousand pounds. His color
was for the most part brown, but his back and
the top of his head appeared nearly white. He
was of the species called by the hunters " silver-
tipped grizzly;" and as the sun was shining very
brightly directly upon his back, the reflection was
such as to give it a silvery-white appearance. He
was evidently trying to make up his mind whether

to come down to us and take his lunch, or betake
himself off up the mountain, — or, as the local
phrase has it, "pull his freight." I had not
thought of the bear's attacking us, though I had
wondered at the Appalachian's coolness, but now
the beast was growling and snapping. Suddenly
my companion suggested, "Suppose he should de-
cide to come and take us." Then I proposed that
I go for the other plates, and that he get his shot-
gun, our only weapon, at the same time, and load
it with buckshot. "That would not be of much
use," he answered; "but we can do one thing.
Here, take this knife!" and he drew a large
butcher-knife from his belt and handed it to me.
"If he turns on us, I will wait till his nose
touches the muzzle of the gun before I let him
have it, and you must do the best you can for
yourself with the knife; this will be our only
salvation, but it will take lots of nerve to await
the proper moment to shoot." Our motions were
so lively that when we got back to our position
by the camera, the bear had decided to move off,
and was soon out of sight behind a ridge, giving
a sort of snort as he turned away. Our fear was
now that he would run down the mountain to
where the horses and mule were tethered and
stampede them. If the animals should get a sight

of the bear, they would break their legs or necks
in trying to escape.   This catastrophe must be
averted at all hazards, for without the pack mule
we could never carry the camera and plates back
to camp before nightfall, and a night at this elevation, without blankets, would be horrible.   We
started at a brisk run over the rocks, hoping to
head him off.   But he travelled so rapidly that
before we saw him again he had covered a great
distance in a circle around us, and was about
three hundred feet below our position, crossing a
large snow-field, and luckily headed away from
the horses.   He stopped, turned, and looked at us.
Standing out on the white snow-field, with steep
ledges and jagged cliffs rising high in the background, his figure was certainly very picturesque.
It was impossible to photograph him, as he was so
far below us ; so my companion asked, —

"Shall I give him a shot ?"

" Pepper him," I responded.

" He may turn on us."

" Pepper him," I said again.

Bang went the gun, and the beast jumped.
Bang ! another charge of buckshot followed, and
the bear gave another leap forward, although the
effect of the shot was probably no more upon him
than the cut of a whip would have been if given

CREVASSE ON THE HALLETT GLACIER.

near at hand. However, the shot so accelerated his gait that he probably reached Wyoming in a very short time, for he went up the side of the mountain on a run, and was over the top of the ridge and out of sight in ten minutes. I watched him for a moment on the ground glass of the camera, and his figure looked like that of a rat running up a wall. This quickness of motion in a beast of such bulk was marvellous; for later in the day it took us over an hour to gain an equal height, climbing over similar rocks. One can judge how utterly powerless we should have been if the conditions had been reversed and we had been chased by the bear.

The bear being disposed of, we returned to the glacier and roped ourselves together for an investigation of the surface of the ice, using a forty-foot lariat for the purpose, so that we had about twenty feet of rope between us. Then we crossed the snow to the big crevasse. This was fifteen feet wide in some places, and twenty to thirty feet deep, and large icicles hung down from the upper edges. After securing photographs of this, we went back to the rocks, where the Appalachian threw off the rope and separated himself from us to climb the final peak by the ledges. Our leader and I tied ourselves

together again, and began the ascent to the ridge
by the glacier.

In Switzerland I had been guided over many
glaciers, and on one occasion had had the sensation of dangling on the
edge of a crevasse
into which I had

fallen; but never before had I led in crossing
a large snow-field, or assumed any responsibility.
The crossing of this glacier looked easy and simple, and one not accustomed to ice-work would
have probably laughed at the idea of using a
rope; but my experience told me that the crevasse, which seemed to end abruptly, probably
extended under the smooth snow for a long distance, and we might strike it or some other cleft

in the ice in any part of the glacier that we might cross. And then there was our leader's former adventure, to which I have already alluded. He was all alone, and ascending on the north side, trying to reach the curious shafts which stand as sentinels over that part of the ice. He was getting along all right, when, suddenly, he broke through the bridge of a hidden crevasse. Luckily the ice was firm at the rim on both sides, so that he held up by his elbows and managed to extricate himself. Safely out, he ran down the mountain, determined never to venture on the snow again without help.

We had no ice-axe. The snow was in the condition of *névé*, and very firm. I used my camera tripod for a feeler, and often could send it down deep in treacherous places; but we kept to a sort of *aréte*, and by stamping foot-holes made some progress. It was very slow, however, as every step must be made, and the incline grew steeper as we advanced. If the snow had been in a more icy condition, we could never have reached the ledges without an axe, and as it was we had to make detours to avoid glare ice. From the summit of the *aréte* we jumped over a suspicious bit of ice to the rocks, and congratulated ourselves that we were the first to tread upon these upper snows.* The ledges we found very narrow and broken up into towers and spires. The west side of the peak was an indescribably wild scene, such as I had never beheld; there were precipices and gorges, masses of rock and bowlders, smooth cliffs, rough-hewn towers, and below us several thousand feet was a gem of a mountain park, with a silver stream winding through it for miles down to the Poudre. Encircling the whole were snow-clad mountains of the Rabbit Ear and Medicine Bow Ranges, and beyond was the Park Range, filling the western horizon with its mountains piled upon mountains. Part of the wonder and delight of the scene was caused by the fact that we were looking upon an almost unknown land as we gazed into the west. The meadows at our feet, walled in by high mountains, are very difficult to get into with pack animals; hence over and among the far mountains there is not a settlement until Utah is reached.

Unlike some of the difficult Swiss peaks, there

---

* After our return to Estes Park, our party spoke of the glacier as the "Mummy Glacier;" but now I am disposed, with Professor Stone of the College of Colorado, who visited it later in the season, to call it "Hallett Glacier." "Mount Hallett" has its name from the same gentleman, having been so christened by Dr. E. O. Otis, of Boston, and the writer, when on its summit in July, 1887.

is always some easy way of access to the high
crests of the Rocky Mountains; but there is hard
climbing to be found, if that is sought. To any
mountaineer in search of such work, I would suggest that he ascend the Mummy glacier by an
arête on the north side to the point where the
shafts of rock are standing, then descend the
mountain to the deep glen below, being careful to
take provisions for two days from camp. After
exploring the valley at its upper limit, let him
ascend the west peak of the Mummy from that
side directly to the summit, and I fancy he will
have need of steadiness of head and strength of
limb.

We began to make the remainder of the climb
of the peak by the broken ledges, and found our
way difficult. The rocks, broken and shattered,
afforded poor hold, and if once they gave way,
went spinning to the lake below with a whir and
a crash that made us realize what would be the
result should we fall from these heights. We had
to help each other with boosts and pulls; for
sometimes there were no firm rocks within reach,
as we felt for them over the edges of platforms
above us. It was not easy to get the gun and
camera up; so finally, after passing the edge of
the ice, which was too treacherous to venture

upon at this point, we were forced to take the face of the mountain, by which we had an easy route to the summit.

The rocks on the top of the Mummy have an entirely different appearance from those of any other summit in the Rocky Mountains on which I have stood. On Pike's Peak, Bald Mountain, Long's Peak, Table Mountain, and on many of the lesser peaks, the slabs of granite are strewn around or heaped up in piles, while here there is little debris, for the rocks are arranged in laminæ with edges up, and present a saw-like appearance; the mountain drops off on all sides, excepting the ridge to the northwest, in noble ledges flanked by massive towers.

We were more than an hour upon the summit; the atmosphere was of rare transparency, and the view seemed limitless. Mountain ranges far into Wyoming were clearly seen; Pike's Peak rose in the south, and peaks farther away to the southwest; but here, as from the ledges below, the chief joy was in looking toward the sierras of the west. This was the only peak upon which we had not found a cairn, and I doubt if it had ever been climbed before.

As we were ascending the glacier a Rocky Mountain eagle swooped down over the ridge, but seeing us he soared up over the top of our peak, and while we were on the summit, was circling over us at a great height, probably at an elevation of 20,000 feet above sea-level. It would be a curious fact to learn at how great an elevation a bird of that size and weight could sustain itself

by flight ; for notwithstanding its lightness as compared with its size, it seems as if it would drop like a piece of cotton in an exhausted tube.

It was four o'clock when we left the summit, and ran down the face of the peak to where we had left our traps and extra plates. Collecting these, we walked to the north side of the glacier and climbed about half-way up. Part of the south side of the glacier is in shadow early in the afternoon, and on that account is very smooth and firm, while the north end is exposed to the sun's rays from early morning till much later in the afternoon; consequently, the heat has so melted the upper snows that the water runs down and causes the deep grooves seen in Plate VI. The surface of all the large ice-fields about Estes Park presents this grooved, or ribbed, structure.* While we had been examining the formation and shape of the curious ridges of snow, the sun had been obscured by high drifting clouds. Suddenly it came out with dazzling brightness, and we beheld a remarkable shadow profile cast upon the

---

* Since writing the above, my attention has been called to a description of the surface of the snow of the Mount Lyell Glacier, in California, which proves that running water is not the first cause in forming the troughs. In the case of the great ice-field, however, the grooves are " in a direction at right angles to the slope." According to Mr. J. T. Gardiner, formerly of the Geological Survey, "the transverse ridges or blades are produced by the *action of sun on wind ripples.* During the winter the wind blows mainly down the cañon, and the loose snow is drifted into wind ripples; during the summer, when neither rain nor snow falls for many months, the snow is greatly wasted, but more in the troughs than on the crests, on account of the reverberation of heat within the troughs." — PROF. JOSEPH LeCONTE, *American Journal of Science and Arts,* 1873, vol. v., 3d series.

pure white snow by the sculptured rocks. At first it was a startling apparition, and we stood there transfixed with awe as we gazed upon it, shading our eyes with our hands. The length of the profile traced on the snow by the varying shadow was fully a hundred feet. The lines were clearly defined. Of course it can only be seen at a certain hour on sunny afternoons. The day is far distant when throngs of tourists will stream up the gorge to see the largest ice-field of Colorado, and by that time perhaps the granite rocks will have crumbled away, worn by rain and cracked by frost, and the profile which we saw will have vanished. Meanwhile many will doubtless be glad that we succeeded in securing a photograph of the strange and beautiful scene.

It was now five o'clock. We reluctantly turned away from the glacier, and scrambling over the moraine to the large snow-field where the bear had crossed, we glissaded down for several hundred feet, then took to the rocks, and soon reached our horses and mule. On the way down, we shot seven ptarmigans. We reached camp at dark in a very tired condition, but a cup of strong coffee so revived us that in an hour we were contentedly lying before the blaze, the thick hedge of spruce timber at our backs keeping off the strong blasts of wind.   Then we told stories of bear, and stories of elk, and stories of " big-horn," and smoked the pipe of peace.

Spruce firewood will always crack and snap ; and this night the sparks rose high, carried far up by the wild wind, and then whisked down the deep gulch toward the plains.   As I lay there looking at the black line of cliffs surrounding us, and then into the dancing flames, I thought of camp-fires long since burned out, of blazing pines in dark forests, of nights in deserted log-cabins in the West or in the stone-roofed *châlet* in the far-away Alps.   Then from the heights and distance came memories of moraine, crevasse, and *bergschrund*, of expanse of snow, of bowlder waste and the wary " big-horn," of spires of rock and domes of ice, and, loosing my hold on consciousness in this strange chaos, I slipped beneath the canvas and was soon asleep.

YPSILON PEAK FROM DEER MOUNTAIN.

CHAPTER VI.

YPSILON PEAK.

THOUGH making many climbs among the higher peaks and giving much study and investigation to the upper snows, not all of the time of two joyous summers in Estes Park was spent on the mountain-tops, but many days were whiled away in rides, drives, and strolls among the quiet scenes of this beautiful vale. Encircling the shores of Mary's Lake and tracing from afar routes which we had followed into the range, was a delight. We climbed the ledges of little Prospect Mountain, and studied the topography of the valleys at our feet or of the rugged mountains in the west. We galloped over pastures; we forded river and creek. Seemingly inexhaustible are the scenes of pleasure to be found along this beautiful river of Estes Park in its short yet varied course through the mountains. Dashing forth from a dark, deep cañon, tumbling over precipices and ledges, the stream ceases for a space in its hurry, winds gently through the peaceful valley, then

again descends as a rapid through ravines in the
foot-hills, and afterward sluggishly creeps across
the plains to join the Platte.   In one of its little
glens we were shown the last memento of Indian
life existing in the valley, — a "wickyup," or
arbor-wigwam, hidden in the dense aspen growth,
and built of these trees.   It had stood there longer

than the oldest settler knew ; the poles were rot-
ting and falling in, and could have retained their
position but a little while longer ; but alas ! a fire
has since swept through the aspen forest, and the
"wickyup" has been destroyed before its time.
Still more interesting and novel are the scenes to
be met with, or perhaps rather to be ferreted out,

along the banks of the little torrents that flow into the Big Thompson from the north and from the south. One of these streams is Wind River, beautiful to me from many associations. It was on one of those happy days upon its borders that my great interest began in the mountain that I am about to describe.

That day I was in this pretty valley with my wife. We had spent the time lazily near a deserted cabin by the stream. I had been fishing a little. Later we were looking at the mountains, which from here are so beautiful in the west. One great peak with a steep wall facing the east, and a long reclining ridge leading toward the southwest, especially interested us. A large snow-field lay on the eastern face; two glittering bands of ice extended skyward to the ridge of the mountain, forming a perfect Y. My wife said to me, " Its name shall be Ypsilon Peak." So it went forth, and the name was accepted by the dwellers in the valley and by the visitors at the ranches.

I have already described the views from two little mountains, Sheep and Prospect, which are in Estes Park, and separated from the main range by valleys and meadows. There is another elevation, nearer to some of the great peaks, which is well worthy of description, especially in connection with Ypsilon. This is Deer Mountain, a beautiful wooded elevation, with long sweeps of pasture-land reaching from the pine growth down to the

rushing Big Thompson River. Beaver Park is on the southern flanks, and separates it from Eagle Cliff. On the north a narrow valley divides it from the southern ridge of the Black Cañon; and this narrow valley leads into a wide "open"

Gazing at Ypsilon from Deer Mountain.

called Horseshoe Park, which lies between Deer Mountain and the range. Deer Mountain, itself beautiful to look upon, gives charming views of the mountains and valleys. One must traverse its summit, a great square nearly a half-mile broad, from one end to the other in order to obtain the different views ; but each corner is marked by an elevated ledge, from whose summit the perfect outlooks are obtained. It was from one of these ledges, the westernmost, and overlooking that unique valley, Horseshoe Park, that I obtained the finest view of Ypsilon.

The larger parks of Colorado, such as Estes, are beautiful ; but these smaller ones found higher up among the mountains are far more interesting and picturesque. Met with in among the fastnesses of the hills, they can never fail to be a surprise to the traveller, the hunter, or the explorer. They are hidden between steep ridges, which are clothed with dense spruce or pine to their base. In the glade the trees are scattered, as if planted for a park with broad walks between. The water flowing through is no longer a dashing torrent, but a quiet stream, its banks lined with aspens which quiver and rustle in the breeze. Sometimes the narrow glen widens into a vast level stretch, with high peaks walling in the distance and looking down upon fair meadows. Such a valley is Horseshoe Park, and Ypsilon and its rocky spurs block the western sky. The smaller glades found about timber-line on Ypsilon and Hague's Peaks are even more picturesque. This is especially true of those found on the densely wooded slopes of the latter peak, which upon the opposite side is a bare rock and snow waste down to a much lower altitude. In following the ill-defined trail from Estes Park to Lawn Lake, along the slopes of the great peak, struggling up through the forest, the traveller suddenly comes upon such glades at frequent intervals, and it seems as if a deer or elk must surely bound out of the tall luxurious grass into the dark forest.

Never anxious to send me away from her side into the mountains, the sponsor of Ypsilon was always desirous that I should ascend this peak ; but the summer vacation of 1887 passed away, and it still remained unclimbed. During this last summer, however, the not difficult but very interesting feat was accomplished.

Thursday, August 9, a camping outfit was packed in Ferguson's stage ; and our party, consisting of Mr. Hallett, Mr. Gilman, Mr. George W. Thacher, Mr. J. R. Edmands, Prof. C. E. Fay, and the writer, started for Horseshoe Park to attempt Ypsilon Peak. Mr. Gilman and myself rode horses, which were to be used as pack animals on our arrival in Horseshoe Park. We left Ferguson's ranch at 9.30 A. M., and reached the end of the road at 11.30. There we unloaded the wagon and sent it home, packed the two horses with the necessary outfit, and turning to the right followed an old trail by the side of a creek which flows from Lawn Lake. We lunched in a park where there was feed for the horses, and higher up at four o'clock forded the creek under some difficulties, the operation consuming half an hour. After leaving the ford, there was no trail; so Mr. Hallett led the procession with axe in hand, and was obliged to cut and hew right and left.

Near Camp Ypsilon.

With our faces now turned directly toward Ypsilon Peak, and several hundred feet above a brook which flows from its snows, we worked our way over the side of a great ancient moraine for three hours, and on the banks of the stream found a suitable camping-spot at dark. I acted as commissary and cook, but fear that my comrades were not over and above pleased with the very plain fare. We passed the night under cover of canvas, rubber, and blankets; we did not carry a tent. With the exception of one of our number, we all slept well.

In the morning we left camp at 7.20, — at first in a body, but, as is generally the case with such a large party, we were soon scattered all over the flanks of Mount Fairchild, over the top of which we intended to go. Mr. Hallett carried my sensitized plates, — a heavy load. I lugged the camera, and in addition to this burden was troubled with a very lame foot, and had little hope of standing on the summit of Ypsilon that day. Mr. Edmands soon made direct for the summit of Fairchild, which he reached at 10.55; while the rest of us bore to the right in order to gain a ridge, by following which we thought we should obtain good views the whole morning long. We kept nearly together, Messrs. Fay and Hallett arriving first on the ridge at 8.15. At that point I took pictures of Ypsilon, and higher up obtained fine views of Hague's Peak and the west peak of the Mummy Range. The deeply furrowed precipitous sides of the former peak, rising nearly three thousand feet above the timber, were marvellous to behold.

Messrs. Fay, Hallett, and Thacher now went ahead for Fairchild; and Mr. Gilman and I, not being in good condition, determined to skirt that mountain a few hundred feet below the summit. We were soon joined by Mr. Thacher, who was also out of sorts and had given up Fairchild. Luckily we had one canteen of milk and a flask of brandy with us, and constituted ourselves an invalid corps for a short time, when, strange to relate, my lame foot with exercise had become entirely well. Mr. Gilman also had quite recovered from his indisposition; so, leaving our friend to continue a direct high-level route to the notch between Fairchild and Ypsilon, we made straight for the top of the former, over the steepest part of the peak. This enabled me to examine a snow-field in which I had long been interested; but I was disappointed in it. When I came to Estes Park, the first of July, it was a great body of snow, and so shows in photographs taken during that month; but it had steadily decreased, and now, a perfect arrowhead in form and at its minimum in size, the ice was very thin and shallow. At the snow we again changed our plans, thinking that we should be too late to meet our friends on the summit, and bore away around the peak, hoping to head them off. We crossed their path a hundred feet above them, and arrived on the scene at an opportune moment. We had commenced to descend at a rapid gait, when Mr. Gilman shouted, "Look! a bear!" He spied the animal, a great cinnamon, as it was emerging from its lair under a projecting ledge. I shouted to Mr. Hallett, who carried a revolver; and he gave Bruin several shots, all but one of which sounded "click" against the rocks. The bullet that returned no sound we suppose lodged in bear meat. Like the grizzly which we met last year on Mummy Mountain, this bear seemed bound for Wyoming, and soon disappeared beyond the sky-line of the mountain; but he gave us lots of fun for a few minutes.

We reached the notch at 12.50 P. M., and there joining Mr. Edmands we began on the lunch. Mr. Thacher soon came in, and reported having seen two young cinnamon bears playing on ledges below him. The bear question was getting serious.

At 1.30 P. M. Messrs. Edmands, Hallett, and Fay started for Ypsilon's crest, which they reached at 2.25. Mr. Thacher started down through a gorge for camp, which I considered a very heroic action; for my part I never should have ventured through that country alone and unarmed. Mr. Gilman and I spent some time selecting view-points and taking photographs, using up most of the plates. The views from the notch are very fine, especially toward the west. Starting for Ypsilon at two o'clock, we followed the route taken by the others, which led up the gradual western slope of the mountain, and reached the summit at 3.10. We found the topographer busy taking angles; but all his labor was for naught, on account of the disturbance caused by the presence of magnetic iron in the rocks. Although the day was perfect for an expedition in the mountains, the breeze was a little too fresh on the highest rocks; so we all dropped down under a ledge on the east face, and scanned with the field-glass the gorges below.

Ypsilon from above is even finer than from below. The snow gullies which form the long lines converging together at the base, which give the peak its name, cut deep into the mountain's flanks, and have formed miniature cañons. Weird shapes of snow cling to nooks which are sheltered from the sun. One cornice had a big hole in it, as if a cannon-ball had passed through. But the great point of interest is the steep character of the whole northeastern face. Numerous lakes were

visible below, between us and our camp; some
were perched on high moraines far away from the
base of the peak; while straight down and over
two thousand feet below, immediately at the base
of the cliffs, we saw two large ones which were
walled in by dikes. All the great peaks in the
neighborhood have these characteristic glacial
lakelets. The debris seems to have been swept
away from the exit end, though great blocks lie
on the side.

In a short time we went to the point near
where the left snow couloir begins, and hurled
off big bowlders, imagining that we could send
them into the water below. Only one thing pre-
vented: we could not find any rocks tenacious
enough to hold together. All were reduced to fragments before they reached the smooth surface of
the lake.

The three who first arrived on the summit
soon left us, and following the ridge descended
the next peak south on their way to camp. After
parting with these companions we returned to the
summit of Ypsilon and commenced to erect a
cairn, but the rocks being too heavy to handle
easily, we gave it up. As the wind had died
down a little, we spread out a map on the rocks,
and with aid of compass identified many points of

interest; but soon abandoned that simply to take in the glorious view. Long's Peak with its grand tower never looked nobler. The mountains in Estes Park were but his little foot-hills. The moraine in Willow Park, the smaller ones in Horseshoe, and the still larger one, which above our camp led down towards Horseshoe Park, were very prominent features in the near landscape. The imposing rocky face of Hague's Peak cut off the northern horizon. Past the turrets of the west peak of the Mummy Range we saw the ice of the summit of Hallett Glacier. Then for the first time I realized why that great mass of snow exceeded all others in the Front Range. Placed near the summit of a peak 14,000 feet in height, it lies in such a cold region that this alone prevents little waste from melting.

The view toward the west is magnificent. It must be remembered that this district is yet in a wild state. Let not the reader think when he looks at the map and sees places noted, such as "Lulu," "Michigan City," that it means much. In many cases such dots mark but the site of deserted mining-camps or lonely ranches. "Moraine," for example, in Estes Park, given place on the map in large letters, is in reality one ranch, Sprague's, with a few cottages for summer visitors.

Perhaps two or three members of the family at the most remain at the ranch during the winter months. Grand County, whose mountains we gazed upon, contains some 2,000 square miles, and had at the last census a population of 417 persons. These mostly dwell in the lower part of Middle Park; so it may be imagined that very few human beings were in the wide country that we looked upon. Right beneath, a deep upper valley of the Cache la Poudre River separated us from the beautiful rock peak represented in Plate IX. This mountain, like innumerable others dominated over by Upper Grand Valley Peak, was a study in itself. The tapering summit, the white snow-field, the glacial lakelet, were beautiful. What an ice-fall and what a crevasse must once have marked the place where one sees the sudden break in the gradual slopes below the lake! There were scenes such as the camera cannot carry away from mountains like these. Far below in the green valley were dashing brooks, roaring cascades, miles of green meadow and great forest, such as the dwellers on the plains little dream grow in Colorado.

All these things were seen in a few moments, and we began a rapid descent. In half an hour we reached the point near the col where we left

UNNAMED MOUNTAIN WEST OF YPSILON PEAK.

the camera, and hastened down the gorge. Of the three routes to camp followed by our divided party, we suspect that we took the most interesting. Surely there are no finer turrets and pinnacles to be found among the mountains than those which surmount the *arêtes* of Ypsilon on the north. We lingered to take some photographs, but when on the col a gust of wind had struck the camera, and throwing it over had broken the ground glass; so the pictures taken later did not prove to be quite in focus. The

accompanying cut represents the sharply serrated portion of a narrow ridge which descends from the shoulder seen in Plate VIII. on the right of the highest peak of Ypsilon. The heavy mass of snow below the junction of the two arms of the Y, fairly indicated in the plate, lies in a gulch of which this ridge forms the right or northerly wall.

As we descended lower we came upon other beautiful lakes and extensive greenswards. The cliffs above us echoed back many a shout which we sent up among them, for we thought that perhaps our companion of the morning might be waiting for us among some of the ledges. Our way was free from great difficulties until near camp and at dark, when we became involved in the mysteries and miseries of a forest swamp. We divided loads and changed packs; but it seemed to me, whichever I carried, camera or plates, that they were never so heavy before. We got to camp at 7.45 o'clock, and were the last in. Camp-fire that night was an interesting one, as each had a story to tell.

It seems that our leader, by an accident and misunderstanding, became separated from his companions, and getting lower down in the gorges arrived first at camp. The professor, descending a little in front of the topographer at the upper edge of the scrub growth, was very much startled by two large cinnamon bears, which at full speed, and growling, advanced upon him in tandem order. He shouted loudly, and whirled his shining canteen in the air with sufficient energy to change the plans of Bruin, who had probably considered him some small game. The one in advance, now within twenty feet, turned so quickly in his tracks that he almost knocked over Ursa Minor, following at his heels. Their appearance was for a moment ludicrous, and tended to neutralize the sensation of fright which the beasts had at first excited. Mr. Edmands hurried to the scene, of which the two gentlemen remained masters; for the animals, after getting themselves together, disappeared into the timber.

Our camp was also a merry one; we knew no sadness. We had been upon a beautiful mountain, had met with adventures and no mishaps, and were now safe around a blazing fire within the circle of whose rays neither bear nor mountain lion would dare to venture.

CHAPTER VII.

OUR party for a grand trip to the Hallett Glacier, returning over Hague's Peak, consisted of four persons, all of whom were connected with the expedition to Ypsilon. It was a question whether we should camp at Horseshoe Park or in the Black Cañon, but at last we chose the latter. We decided to take a wagon as far as possible, and so carry a tent. We also made up our minds to dispense with pack animals, and make a long day of it.

We left Ferguson's at two o'clock P. M., August 14, reached the end of the wagon-road on the south bank of the stream at a quarter before four, and getting our traps across the river pitched our fly-tent under some pines. While the others were doing the hard work of making camp, I shirked duty, and ascending the slope on the south side of the cañon took a number of photographs of the walls opposite. Three towering rocks mark the highest part of the cañon; below, the

MOUNT FAIRCHILD AND HAGUE'S PEAK OVER MARY'S LAKE.

summits are dome-shaped, and far down, near
the entrance, two sculptured figures stand out
from the parapet, appearing almost exactly like
two great owls. These remarkable rocks interested me ; but I was soon obliged to leave them,
for I had only been gone from camp an hour be-

fore it commenced
to rain. The rainy
season was sup-
posed to be over;
but this night
gave such suppo-
sition the lie, for
the storm contin-
ued all through
the dark hours.
The fly-tent shed
most of the water,
and we slept
soundly and were
kept dry. This was the only occasion on which
we used a tent in expeditions among the mountains ; and it was very fortunate that we brought
one this day.

Our camp was certainly a luxurious one ; such
living as we had, if continued, would soon spoil
one for hard trips ; but it was a reaction against

the very simple fare that I, as commissary, had
imposed upon my friends in Camp Ypsilon.   Another acted in this capacity in the memorable
camp in the Black
Cañon, and course
followed   course, —
oat-meal, roasted po-
tatoes, toast, steak,
etc., till at eleven
o'clock draughts of

chocolate ended the supper, and pipes were brought
out.   The commissary also did the proper thing in
the morning, — built a fire before we were awake,

and at five o'clock whispered gently in our ear, "Coffee," which we drank before getting up.

The day dawned so dark and rainy that it was seven o'clock before we decided to start. One of our number had brought a horse, on which he proposed to ride as far as the trail led up the cañon. This was a great gain to the rest of us also, as he carried the lunch. We started off at a terrific pace, knowing that we must hurry. The pedestrians got very wet, but the horseman was so thoroughly soaked and chilled that at half-past nine he decided to turn back. He had received all the water from the wet branches that he had ridden through, while the rest of us were only wet below the knees.

Mr. Edmands, Professor Fay, and I kept on toward Lawn Lake, which we reached at quarter before eleven. This lake is certainly a marvellous sheet of water, situated in a valley about 10,700 feet above the sea. It is over half a mile long, has beautiful grassy slopes on all sides, and fine groves of spruce near its banks. High above, on the south, loom the crags of Mount Fairchild. The precipices of Hague's Peak rise three thousand feet above one on the north, and at the end of the valley are the buttresses of the west peak of the Mummy.

Summit of Hague's Peak.

We made for this mountain, our route sometimes leading through a maze of bowlders, and
then up steep grassy slopes; then again over level

greenswards where innumerable rills wandered. Among the rocks we saw two badgers, the only animals larger than conies that we met this day. They seemed alone in this wild solitary basin, and we did not disturb them with a shot.

We passed two lakes at the base of the peaks of Mount Fairchild, lunched near the notch between that mountain and the Mummy, and soon began our ascent.

It is rarely that the climber in the Rockies meets with much difficulty in ascending the accessible sides of the peaks. I have already pointed out the fact that an easy route is generally found to the summits; but the illustrations which refer to Long's Peak and Ypsilon Peak show conclusively that one face on each of these peaks is absolutely inaccessible. On this day we seemed to have struck the rocks on the Mummy at a place which gave us the only bit of difficult scrambling that we found during the summer. If they had been a little more difficult, we should have been obliged to make a long detour. When our work commenced the weather was fair, and we had clear views of the valley below, and of the surrounding peaks; but as we got higher up, a dense fog settled down upon our peak, and later snow fell, making the rocks quite slippery. To select an easy route was impossible; the ledges became barely practicable. Fortunately the dip of the strata was in our favor, the rocks were pretty firm, and we mounted higher and higher. The storm added to the weirdness of the situation; splintered crags appeared before us like the weathered towers of ancient fortresses. Overhanging rocks forced us to edge around on narrow ledges. Seen through fog, rain, or snow-flakes, the heights above were magnified, and the Mummy, which from the valleys seems as if in repose, now showed itself an angry mountain. Lover as I am of clear, distant panoramic views, yet I would not like to have missed this day's experience. We finally overcame all difficulties; but on gaining the summit, denser clouds encompassed us, and snow-squalls rushed over the peak. The temperature was 34° above zero. Very soon we started down toward the glacier. The clouds grew thicker and denser, and we could see but a little way before us. After descending to what I thought the proper distance I hesitated, for I knew we must be within a few hundred feet of the ice, and also realized that in the obscuring fog it would be very easy to go a little too far to the left, and be landed in the Cache la Poudre valley. In a few minutes the clouds lifted a little, and I recognized

the snowfield where the grizzly crossed the year
before.

I glanced to the left and waited for the uncov-
ering of the great ice-field. We had to linger but
a moment; a sudden rush of wind dissolved the
mist, or bore it up the steep slopes, and the weird
ice-field lay before us, its summit line of snow
high above us clearly cut

against a fog-
bank, and great yawning crevasses even with our
eyes. It was a supreme moment to me, for I had
talked so much to my friends of this ice-field and
its wonders, that I feared their disappointment;
and now when their exclamation came forth,
"Wonderful!" I was exceedingly gratified.

The situation had changed but little in a year.

Some of the rocky spires had fallen ; but the general line of cliffs stood intact, even the nose of the profile rock had not varied in shape. The crevasses were narrower but longer, and extended nearly across the field. The blocks of ice were much larger in the lake, and were deeply grooved both on the upper and lower surfaces. Thin pieces of ice were also floating there, side by side with the icebergs, clearly illustrating the difference between the frozen lake-water and masses which had fallen from the glacier. The tops of the bergs were like crusted snow, while the under surfaces were clear blue ice. The temperature of the water was 34°, the same as that of the air on the summit of the peak. ` Our altitude was about 13,000 feet.

We left the base of the ice at about three o'clock, reached a deep notch between the two peaks of the Mummy Range in an hour, and immediately tackled the steep though not difficult side of Hague's Peak. We reached the top in an hour and a half ; so late in the day, it was rather cold, but we thoroughly enjoyed the view. Magnetic properties of the summit rocks again interfered with our topographer's work in taking angles.

Isolated from the Front Range by deep valleys,

this peak is certainly well calculated to serve as a view-point from which to observe the surrounding mountains. It was a delight to me, as I lay on the rocks, to look at the many peaks that I had climbed in the range, and recall incidents in the different ascents. But two elevations of importance remained for me to scale in the long line extending from Long's Peak to our mountain, one of which, fortunately, I am able to describe in the concluding chapter.

As viewed from the valleys, and from many points in Estes Park, it had always seemed to me that the west peak of the Mummy Range was a trifle higher than Hague's Peak; but when on the former summit the year before, it seemed as if Hague's was the higher of the two; and now, as we looked back at the west peak, it certainly did appear higher than our position, and the barometric record of the day gave it about two hundred feet the advantage.

The lateness of the hour did not allow us to linger long over the view, and the knowledge of the character of the blind trail which we must follow after reaching the cañon made us look anxiously at the declining sun. It was five o'clock when we turned from the summit, and started at a rapid gait down the precipitous sides of Hague's Peak. We were not much fatigued by our long tramp, so we sprang lightly from bowlder to bowlder when among rocks, and ran swiftly over the lower grassy stretches and down through the timber that clothes the slope above the trail; yet darkness overtook us in the forest lower down, and we had a struggle among its mazes. We lost all trace of trail, and only knew of our emergence from the cañon by our voices ceasing to return echoes from the walls above. Fortunately, when we reached our camp, a wagon was waiting for us; all the traps had been packed up, and an hour later saw us at Ferguson's.

As the result of the experience of three expeditions, perhaps it would be well to state the best way of visiting the four peaks in this neighborhood; namely, Ypsilon Peak, Mount Fairchild, and the two summits of the Mummy Range. A passable trail leads up Black Cañon to Lawn Lake, and near it there is good feed for horses. A camp could be pitched there the first day; Ypsilon Peak and Mount Fairchild ascended on the second; Hallett Glacier and the two peaks of the Mummy Range on the third; and a leisurely return made to Estes Park on the fourth day.

MOUNT HALLETT TO STONE'S PEAK, FROM DEER MOUNTAIN.

CHAPTER VIII.

THE period of my stay in Estes Park was drawing to a close. I had almost made up my mind to take no more trips among the higher peaks. On the evening of August 17 three of my mountaineering friends left Ferguson's for Lamb's ranch, with the intention of ascending Long's Peak on the following day. I could not well be away from home that night, so could not go with them; but seeing them stride away from us, all my restless qualities were aroused, and I said to our leader, who was standing in the crowd which had gathered to see the climbers off, "Why not start early in the morning and ascend the peak above Willow Cañon? This will be a novel expedition." He assented; though maintaining that it would be a very long day's tramp, and that it would be much better to camp at timber-line. "However, we will try," he said. So in the bright moonlight we went out into the pasture, rounded up the horses and got them into the corral, in order to have them ready for an early start.

At four o'clock the next morning there came a tap at my cabin window.

" Hallett ? "

" Yes ; time to be off."

We were on our horses in half an hour, and were soon riding at a wild gallop toward Willow Cañon.

In Willow Park we disturbed two deer that were feeding in the meadow; they speedily left for the mountains, and we had no time to follow. It was fortunate for us that we took horses for the first part of the journey, for in following the cañon trail we were obliged to ford the river several times. At quarter-past seven we reached the end of the trail. Tying the horses, with no other burden than a canteen of milk, lunch, barometer, and field-glass, we pushed on and up through the forest. It was a delight to be free from heavy weights; and much as I needed the camera on many occasions that day, I do not regret having left it behind.

Very soon we hit upon an old elk-trail, which was of much use for a while. In it we observed fresh tracks of a mountain lion. We reached the junction of Fern River and the Willow Cañon stream at eight o'clock, and then followed an unnamed creek, the sources of which we were to know better later in the day. We soon crossed it to the right, and climbed steep wooded slopes till, at ten o'clock, we reached timber-line (altitude 11,100 feet). Here we attacked a ridge, which we hoped, and not in vain, would lead us to the main peak whose side was marked by a large snow-field. Our route lay over the summit of three very steep mi-

Playground of the Big-horn.

nor peaks, and we were often brought face to face with precipices, and obliged to change our course. In among ledges were frequent grass-plots, where we noticed signs of big-horn. Rounding a crag we suddenly startled a noble ram,— a perfect specimen, with magnificent curling horns. He leaped from rock to rock, and disappeared, only to reappear on successive ledges to take a look at us. After gaining a considerable height above us, he seemed to take courage, made longer rests, and once stopped to rub himself against a projecting ledge. We had several opportunities to examine him with the field-glass. He soon reached the summit of a ridge, and standing for a moment on the crest, his beautiful form projected against the sky-line, he gave us a parting glance and was not seen again. We moved on, and immediately another ram jumped up in front of us. This time so great was the bewilderment of the animal that he did not think to go up the mountain, his natural way of escape, but rushed down a narrow gorge which ended in a precipice of a thousand feet, and paused on the outer rim of the dizzy cliff. A pistol-shot would have killed him. We could have knocked him over with a big stone, but of what use such cruelty? We could never have carried home the trophy. He glanced at us a moment, and his figure neatly balanced was a most interesting spectacle. The next instant he jumped to a ledge under the tower which we stood upon, rounded it in two skilful bounds where we could not have passed, and escaped down the mountain.

Reasoning that more of the animals might be feeding on the grassy slopes of the opposite sides of the mountain, we were on our guard against more surprises. With the wind dead ahead we climbed very carefully, and as we surmounted each ridge, we kept our bodies hidden, and worked our way very carefully for two hours, crawling in many places, till we reached a point where only two peaks remained between us and the snow-field. Creeping to a notch we peered over a broken ledge, and were rewarded for our long fatiguing stalk by beholding twelve big-horn quietly feeding or resting only a hundred yards below us. The first ram had evidently gone higher up the mountain, so had not alarmed the flock. Quickly and stealthily slipping over the ridge, we slid behind a bowlder, and were able to observe with a powerful field-glass the family life and movements of these wild animals perfectly unaware of our presence. The flock consisted of eight ewes, two yearlings, and two very young ones. The latter we frequently observed in the act of sucking. An old ewe lying on an eminence seemed to be doing guard-duty. The flock moved but slowly ; we noticed some getting up and others lying down. It was an hour before the group passed out of sight around the side of the mountain.

Notwithstanding our proximity to the big-horn that day, it would have been impossible to have photographed them, even if we had brought a camera; for, on account of the roughness of the ground, I could not have got the instrument in place quick enough to catch the rams in a good position; again the flock was too far removed, and their color, a dusky brown, too nearly that of the rocks among which they were moving, to secure clearness of outline in a picture. Seventy-five yards is about the limit of distance at which a picture of animals of such size, that is, about six feet long and three feet six inches high, could successfully be obtained.

At two o'clock we were on our way once more, and half an hour later, near the top of what I call for convenience " Peak No. 3," a fierce snow-storm obliged us to take refuge under a ledge. The whirling snow-flakes blinded us so that we could not face the storm. The temperature was about 45° Fahrenheit above zero. In a half-hour the weather cleared about us, and the storm drove towards Long's Peak. Now we saw below us a beautiful rainbow thrown against the long range north of Willow Cañon. The arch rested entirely on the mountain, no part of it reflected on the sky, — a necessary result of such a phenomenon at that time of day. The barometer gave 13,100 feet as the altitude of " Peak No. 3."

At three o'clock in a violent wind, which had followed the snow-storm, we stood upon " Peak No. 2," altitude 13,130 feet. The gale, however, soon subsided, after clearing the air of clouds, and our view was unobstructed. A light covering of snow lay over the great range; but the power of the sun was so great, that in an hour all the snow was melted, and no one would have believed that there had been such a squall.

The main peak was now within our grasp; but being in no hurry to bag it, we first strolled to the west edge of the mountain, and looked down into a beautiful green valley whose stream is a tributary of the Poudre. I do not doubt that elk can be found in this valley; surely it is just the place for them. I had long wished to stand at this point, in order to examine with a field-glass two large snow-fields which, when seen from the summit of Ypsilon Peak, I had thought might prove to be of a glacial nature. From this nearer view-point they showed clearly their true character; they were simply large shallow snow-fields.

The ragged and wild appearance of the mountain tops surprised me; and this view, now comparatively unknown, is destined, I think, to become famous. One sharp rock-peak directly to the southwest of Stone's Peak deserves the attention of mountaineers.

As we turned and climbed towards the summit of Stone's Peak, rising above the peaks to the west and now at our backs, we often stopped, faced about, and looked at them. Clark's Peak, in the Medicine Bow Range, is a beauty from this point. Specimen Mountain, recognized by the kite-shaped snow-field near its flat top, was especially interesting. This mountain, as well as a number of similar peaks around it, has been the scene of volcanic disturbance, or, as Lamb of Long's Peak says, "of a blow-out." Its sides are said to be covered with pumice.

Now came the great event of the day. We had nearly gained the top of the peak, and were crossing a ridge with our faces turned toward the south, when there came in view a large snow-field that no one would have expected to find in such a position. Mr. Hallett exclaimed, "There's a frozen lake for you!" Then both of us cried, "A glacier!"

At quarter-past three we were on the highest rocks of Stone's Peak. I at once read my barometer, and took compass bearings. The altitude was found to be 13,500 feet. The west peak of

Mummy Mountain lay due north; Hague's Peak
15° east of north; and Long's Peak 10° south of
east. The observations were made with all possible haste, as no time was to be lost if the marvellous snow-field was to be reached. At four o'clock
we were off. We realized that we were imperil-
ling, if not life and limb, at least our comfort and
the peace of mind of friends at the ranch, in thus
launching out in a direction away from home at
that time of day instead of turning toward it;
but our excitement was too great to listen to the
counsel of prudence. Though foreseeing that we
might be headed off by some cañon wall in taking
an unknown line of descent, we thought that we
could still make timber-line at least by dark,
build a fire, and keep warm.

Our descent was rapid. We went over the top of
two rocky needles and reached the slopes of the
peak which bore the snow-field without having
gone below the level of the foot of the ice; but alas!
here we were turned from our nearly direct high-
level route by a sheer wall, and were obliged to
drop down several hundred feet, then reascend to
the same altitude. The whole descent and ascent
was made at a running gait, and the ice was
gained at five o'clock. The altitude was 12,100
feet.

Immediately before reaching the semi-frozen lake that lay at the base of the ice, we skirted the sides of a tarn, then surmounted a dike from the top of which the wonderful snow-slope could be seen from summit to base. It lies on the north face of the mountain, inclined at as steep an angle as will allow of clinging snow. By the east edge it might be possible to ascend the rocks, but on the west side all access is barred, for the snow fills a basin whose walls of rock rise, on that side, smooth and sheer without ledge or cranny. The ice-slope itself could not be climbed without laborious cutting of steps. It is similar in appearance to the snow-field on Table Mountain, but larger and deeper. The evidence that it is of a glacial character rests entirely in the fact that blocks of ice twenty to thirty feet square, and from three to six feet thick, have fallen off into the water, showing that they have been squeezed out by pressure from above. A tongue of ice extended out into the water for perhaps thirty feet, having in it, under water, three large wedge-shaped crevasses, while above the water-line were five similar ones in succession. Some hundreds of feet higher up, on the west side, were several ice-chasms, one that was probably eight feet wide.

The snow-field is not over a quarter of a mile wide, and a thousand feet high. It is a body of *névé* to which there is no trunk except the tongue of ice referred to, which is the result of pressure, and resembles an ice-stream. In comparison with Hallett Glacier it is much steeper, rivals it in the size of the ice-masses that have fallen into the lake, but is inferior to it in the size, though not in the number, of its crevasses.

The cliffs that surround the ice are so smooth and worn that but little debris falls on the snow. A few small stones lay on the west side, and quite a large mass of bowlders rested on the eastern edge, about a hundred feet above the lake. My impression is that any rocks that fall on the ice near the summit are carried down and deposited in the lake.

The top of the dike which walls in the water is free from loose stones. On the lake side, however, it is covered with rocks, and all along the banks of the lake are big bowlders. While I was examining the ice my companion cut his name on a little stick which he carried, and building a cairn on the top of a large rock on the edge of the water, left the stick in the cairn.

Standing upon the dike high above the lake, just before leaving the ice-field, I was surprised to find that I could see a point on Sheep Mountain, where I had stood in July, and there made record of the snow-fields visible, twenty in number. Of these, one situated on Hague's Peak had entirely disappeared, two had diminished to minute white patches, while the remaining seventeen had essentially retained their size. I never should have suspected that this particular ice-field, one of the seventeen, had such great size and depth; but a few days later, when visiting Sheep Mountain, I found that I could see, with the aid of a spy-glass, the large crevasses before referred to.

At half-past five o'clock we began to realize that we must take a return journey, part of it over unfamiliar ground, and must cover a distance that had taken us twelve hours' time to accomplish, — ten hours in actual motion. We got under way. Evidently it was a great day for game, for we started up two badgers the first thing. It was fortunate for us that daylight lasted while we were descending the ledges, for it would have been a hazardous undertaking two hours later. Lower down very steep grass-slopes required care on account of their slipperiness, caused by rain ; but we were able to make very quick time until darkness overtook us in the dense forest and long before we reached the trail. What had been snow in the mountains had been rain in the cañons, and we were wet through.

This unnamed and unexplored cañon rivals in the steepness of its walls many of the famous gorges of Colorado. A grand forest fills it from Willow Park nearly up to the Continental Divide; fires have never ravaged it; it is truly primeval. The noble trees are Engelmann spruce, and for several miles we walked among trees seventy-five feet tall. The ground was mossy and spongy. We kept on "benches" as far as possible, but were continually forced to cross and recross the streams to avoid the ledges and rock-falls which swept down on either side.

At eight o'clock it was very dark, but the nearly full moon appeared above the southeastern walls and gave us some light. Unfortunately from that time on we had to keep on the southerly side of the gorge, and had only reflected light from the opposite walls, but that was better than nothing. We got along best when we could walk on fallen timber that chanced to lie parallel with the river; but when the fallen trees formed a net-work we had to go very slowly, sitting down on the logs and throwing our feet over, at the risk of breaking our legs in many falls. Once my companion turned to me and said, " Are you very tired ? "   I gave the usual answer for such occasions, "Not a bit." "It's lucky for you, then, for we are a long way from the horses."

For the crossing of the torrent we always found a fallen log at hand, which we bravely walked upright, notwithstanding the slippery surfaces. At the final crossing, however, after Hallett had stepped lightly over, I basely straddled the log and used my hands as propellers.

What misery we should have endured that night, if we had not been perfectly well and strong! When we struck the elk-trail I wondered if the mountain lion was still near, and for the tenth time lit my pipe. As my companion remarked, if we had been killed by accident or by wild beasts, none but experienced trailers would ever have been able to find our bodies in the dense forest.

We gained the horses at 10.30 P. M. Finding that it was too dark to ride safely for the first half-hour, we floundered along toward the "open," mounting only to cross the stream. A wild gallop we had when we did reach the meadows, and midnight saw us in our cabins.

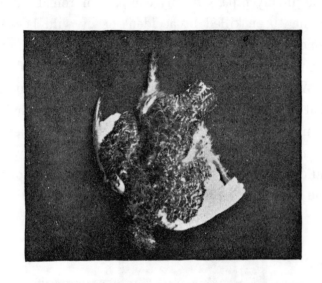

APPENDIX.

A PARTIAL LIST OF PLANTS GROWING IN ESTES PARK, COLORADO.

OBSERVED DURING THE MONTHS OF JULY, AUGUST, AND SEPTEMBER.

Anemone, WIND-FLOWER.
  A. patens, var. Nuttalliana.
  A. cylindrica.
  A. dichotoma.

Thalictrum, MEADOW-RUE.
  T. cornuti.
  T. sparsiflorum.

Ranunculus, BUTTERCUP.
  R. flammula, var. reptans.
  R. sceleratus.
  R. Cymbalaria.
  R. affinis, var. cardiophyllus.
  R. aquatilis, var. trichophyllus.
  R. Nuttallii.
  R. hyperboreus, var. natans.

Caltha, MARSH MARIGOLD.
  C. leptosepala.

Aquilegia, COLUMBINE.
  A. cœrulea.
  A. chrysantha.
  A. brevistyla.

Delphinium, LARKSPUR.
  D. occidentale.

Aconitum, ACONITE.
  A. Columbianum.

Actæa, BANEBERRY.
  A. spicata, var. rubra.

Berberis, BARBERRY.
  B. repens.

Arabis, ROCK CRESS.
  A. Holbœllii.

Cardamine, BITTER CRESS.
  C. cordifolia.

Erysimum.
  E. asperum, var. Arkansanum.

Lepidium, PENNY CRESS.
  L. intermedium.

Viola, VIOLET.
  V. biflora.
  V. palustris.

Silene, CATCHFLY.
  S. Scouleri.
  S. acaulis.

Saponaria.
  S. Vaccaria.

Lychnis, COCKLE.
  L. montana.

Cerastium, MOUSE-EAR CHICK-WEED.
  C. alpinum, var. Behringianum.

Stellaria, CHICKWEED.
  S. longifolia.

Arenaria, SANDWORT.
  A. capillaris, var. nardifolia.
  A. biflora, var. carnosula.
  A. lateriflora.
Claytonia, SPRING BEAUTY.
  C. Chamissonis.
  C. Caroliniana, var. sessilifolia.
  C. megarrhiza.
Sidalcea, MALLOW.
  S. candida.
Linum, FLAX.
  L. perenne.
Geranium, CRANESBILL.
  G. Richardsoni.
  G. incisum.
  G. cæspitosum.
Ceanothus, NEW JERSEY TEA.
  C. velutinus.
  C. Fendleri.
Acer, MAPLE.
  A. glabrum.
Thermopsis.
  T. montana.
Lupinus, LUPINE.
  L. Burkei.
Trifolium, CLOVER.
  T. dasyphyllum.
  T. nanum.
Oxytropis.
  O. Lamberti.
  O. Lamberti, var. sericea.
Physocarpus, NINE-BARK.
  P. opulifolia.
Holodiscus.
  H. discolor, var. dumosa.
Rubus, RASPBERRY.
  R. deliciosus.
  R. strigosus.
Purshia.
  P. tridentata.
Dryas.
  D. octopetala.

Geum, AVENS.
  G. macrophyllum.
  G. rivale.
  G. Rossii.
Potentilla, FIVE-FINGER.
  P. arguta.
  P. dissecta.
  P. supina.
  P. gracilis.
  P. Hippiana.
  P. effusa.
  P. fruticosa.
  P. Anserina.
Sibbaldia.
  S. procumbens.
Agrimonia, AGRIMONY.
  A. Eupatoria.
Rosa, ROSE.
  R. blanda.
  R. Arkansana.
Amelanchier, JUNE-BERRY.
  A. alnifolia.
Saxifraga, SAXIFRAGE.
  S. flagellaris.
  S. chrysantha.
  S. cæspitosa.
  S. cernua.
  S. bronchialis.
  S. rivularis.
  S. Jamesii.
  S. punctata.
Mitella, MITRE-WORT.
  M. pentandra.
Heuchera, ALUM-ROOT.
  H. bracteata.
Parnassia, GRASS OF PARNAS-
  SUS.
  P. parviflora.
Jamesia.
  J. Americana.
Ribes, CURRANT, GOOSEBERRY.
  R. cereum.

Sedum, STONE-CROP.
S. Rhodiola.
S. rhodanthum.
S. stenopetalum.

Epilobium, WILLOW-HERB.
E. spicatum.
E. coloratum.

Gayophytum.
G. racemosum.

Œnothera, EVENING PRIM-
ROSE.
Œ. biennis.
Œ. albicaulis.
Œ. cæspitosa.

Mentzelia.
M. multiflora.

Opuntia.
O. Missouriensis.

Ligusticum, LOVAGE.
L. apiifolium.
L. montanum.

Linnæa, TWIN-FLOWER.
L. borealis.

Galium, BEDSTRAW.
G. boreale.

Valeriana, VALERIAN.
V. edulis.

Brickellia.
B. grandiflora.

Liatris, BLAZING STAR.
L. punctata.
L. scariosa.

Grindelia, GUM-PLANT.
G. squarrosa.

Chrysopsis, GOLDEN ASTER.
C. villosa.

Aplopappus.
A. Parryi.

Bigelovia, RAYLESS GOLDEN-
ROD.
B. Douglasii, var. tortifolia.

Solidago, GOLDENROD.
S. humilis.
S. humilis, var. nana.

Aster.
A. oblongifolius, var. rigidulus.
A. lævis.
A. adscendens.
A. foliaceus, var. frondeus.
A. glaucus.

Erigeron, FLEABANE.
E. macranthus.
E. glabellus, var. mollis.
E. compositus.
E. divergens.

Anaphalis, EVERLASTING.
A. margaritacea.

Gnaphalium, EVERLASTING.
G. Sprengelii.
G. strictum.

Rudbeckia, CONEFLOWER.
R. hirta.
R. laciniata.

Helianthus, SUNFLOWER.
H. annuus.
H. pumilus.
H. Nuttallii.

Bahia.
B. chrysanthemoides.

Actinella.
A. depressa.
A. grandiflora.

Gaillardia.
G. aristata.

Achillea, YARROW.
A. Millefolium.

Artemisia, WORMWOOD, SAGE-
BRUSH.
A. frigida.
A. biennis.
A. Norvegica.
A. Ludoviciana.
A. Mexicana.
A. tridentata.

Arnica.
A. cordifolia.
A. latifolia.
A. Parryi.
A. alpina.

Senecio, GROUNDSEL.
S. amplectens.
S. Bigelovii.
S. cernuus.
S. Fremonti.
S. rapifolius.
S. triangularis.
S. serra.
S. crassulus.
S. lugens, var. foliosus.
S. aureus, var. borealis.
S. aureus, var. croceus.
S. Douglasii.

Cnicus, PLUMED THISTLE.
C. Americanus.

Hieracium, HAWKWEED.
H. gracile, var. detonsum.
H. albiflorum.

Prenanthes.
P. racemosa.

Lygodesmia.
L. juncea.

Troximon.
T. glaucum.
T. glaucum, var. dasycephalum.

Lactuca, LETTUCE.
L. pulchella.

Campanula, HAREBELL.
C. uniflora.
C. planiflora.
C. rotundifolia.

Vaccinium, BLUEBERRY.
V. Myrtillus, var. microphyllum.

Arctostaphylos, BEARBERRY.
A. Uva-ursi "Kinnikinnick."

Moneses.
M. uniflora.

Pyrola, WINTERGREEN.
P. minor.
P. secunda.
P. chlorantha.
P. rotundifolia, var. uliginosa.

Chimaphila, PIPSISSEWA.
C. umbellata, "Prince's Pine."

Pterospora, PINEDROPS.
P. andromedea.

Dodecatheon, SHOOTING-STAR.
D. Meadia.

Primula, PRIMROSE.
P. angustifolia.
P. Parryi.

Androsace.
A. Chamæjasme.

Apocynum, INDIAN HEMP.
A. androsæmifolium.

Gentiana, GENTIAN.
G. serrata.
G. barbellata.
G. heterosepala.
G. prostrata.
G. frigida.
G. Parryi.
G. affinis.
G. Bigelovii.

Swertia.
S. perennis.

Frasera.
F. speciosa.

Phlox.
P. Douglasii.

Gilia.
G. gracilis.
G. spicata.
G. pinnatifida.

Polemonium, GREEK VALE-
RIAN, JACOB'S LADDER.
  P. confertum.
  P. confertum, var. mellitum.
  P. humile, var. pulchellum.
  P. cœruleum.

Phacelia.
  P. integrifolia.
  P. sericea.

Echinospermum, STICKSEED.
  E. Redowskii.

Krynitzkia.
  K. Californica.
  K. virgata.

Mertensia, LUNGWORT.
  M. Sibirica.
  M. alpina.

Myosotis, FORGET-ME-NOT.
  M. sylvatica, var. alpestris.

Lithospermum, GROMWELL.
  L. multiflorum.

Pentstemon, BEARD-TONGUE.
  P. glaber.
  P. glaucus, var. stenosepalus.

Chionophila.
  C. Jamesii.

Mimulus, MONKEY-FLOWER.
  M. floribundus.

Synthyris.
  S. alpina.

Veronica, SPEEDWELL.
  V. Americana.
  V. alpina.
  V. peregrina.

Castilleia, PAINTED CUP.
  C. linariæfolia.
  C. pallida.
  C. pallida, var. occidentalis.

Orthocarpus.
  O. luteus.

Pedicularis, LOUSEWORT.
  P. Grœnlandica.
  P. Parryi.
  P. racemosa.
  P. procera.

Aphyllon.
  A. uniflorum.

Utricularia, BLADDERWORT.
  U. vulgaris.

Monarda, HORSE-MINT.
  M. fistulosa.

Brunella.
  B. vulgaris.

Scutellaria, SKULLCAP.
  S. resinosa.
  S. galericulata.

Stachys, WOUNDWORT.
  S. palustris.

Chenopodium, PIGWEED.
  C. capitatum.

Eriogonum.
  E. alatum.
  E. heracleoides.
  E. flavum.

Oxyria, MOUNTAIN SORREL.
  O. digyna.

Polygonum, KNOTWEED.
  P. tenue, var. microspermum.
  P. viviparum.

Shepherdia, BUFFALO-BERRY.
  S. Canadensis.

Betula, BIRCH.
  B. glandulosa.

Alnus, ALDER.
  A. viridis.
  A. incana, var. virescens.

Populus, POPLAR.
  P. tremuloides.
  P. angustifolia.

Habenaria, ORCHID.
  H. obtusata.

Spiranthes, Ladies' Tresses.
  S. Romanzoffiana.

Goodyera, Rattlesnake Plantain.
  G. Menziesii.

Listera.
  L. cordata.

Iris, Blue Flag.
  I. Missouriensis.

Sisyrinchium, Blue - eyed Grass.
  S. mucronatum.

Allium, Onion.
  A. cernuum.

Smilacina, False Solomon's Seal.
  S. amplexicaulis.
  S. stellata.

Lilium, Lily.
  L. Philadelphicum.

Lloydia.
  L. serotina.

Calochortus.
  C. Gunnisoni.

Streptopus.
  S. amplexifolius.

Zygadenus.
  Z. elegans.

Sagittaria, Arrowhead.
  S. variabilis.

CONIFERÆ (Pine Family).

Juniperus, Juniper.
  J. communis, var. alpina.
  J. Virginiana.

Abies, Fir.
  A. subalpina.

Pseudotsuga, Douglas Spruce.
  P. Douglasii.

Picea, Spruce.
  P. Engelmanni.
  P. pungens.

Pinus, Pine.
  P. edulis.
  P. ponderosa, var. scopulorum.
  P. contorta.

LYCOPODINEÆ (Club-mosses).

Selaginella.
  S. rupestris.

Lycopodium.
  L. annotinum.

FILICES (Ferns).

Polypodium vulgare.
Cryptogramme acrostichoides.
Pteris aquilina.

Asplenium Trichomanes.
Phegopteris Dryopteris.
Cystopteris fragilis.
Woodsia Oregana.

EQUISETACEÆ (Horse-tail Family).

Equisetum arvense.

NOTES

Notes are keyed to page and line numbers. For example, 9:9 means page 9, line 9.

Alice Louise Seavey Chapin (?–1888), Frederick Chapin's first wife, who accompanied him to Estes Park in 1887 and 1888. Chapin credits her with the naming of Mount Ypsilon.

PREFACE

9:9. The question of whether Cabeza de Vaca entered any part of the territory that would become New Mexico during his incredible eight-year (1528–36), six-thousand-mile trek westward from the coast of Texas is still debated among historians.

9:14. In 1742, the brothers François and Louis Joseph La Verendrye, traveling west in an attempt to locate a shortcut to the Pacific, came in sight of what they called the "Shining Mountains," probably the Bighorn Mountains of north-central Wyoming.

9:17. All five men greatly enhanced the nation's geographic knowledge of Colorado and the trans-Mississippi West. Meriwether Lewis (1744–1809) and William Clark (1770–1838) were dispatched by Thomas Jefferson in 1804 to investigate the recently acquired Louisiana Purchase. Their expedition provided the first description of the Rocky Mountains, which they crossed to the north of Colorado on their way to the Pacific Ocean. Lieutenant Zebulon M. Pike (1779–1813) was the first official American explorer to enter Colorado. He and his twenty-three-man party sighted Pikes Peak on November 15, 1806, and made an unsuccessful attempt to scale it. Major Stephen H. Long (1784–1864), at the head of a scientific expedition party in search of the sources of the Red River, entered Colorado in late June of 1820 and on the morning of June 30 sighted the Rocky Mountains. Long's party traversed the base of the Front Range from north to south but made no attempt to approach, let alone climb, the peak in Estes Park that would soon bear his name. On July 14, 1820, three members of the Long party did, however, reach the summit of Pikes Peak. Major John C. Fremont (1813–90), the "Pathfinder of the West," led five expeditions into Colorado between 1842 and 1848. His parties explored the headwaters of the Blue, Arkansas, and Platte rivers and entered North, Middle, and South parks.

9:20. Ferdinand V. Hayden (1829–1887), as head of the United States Geological and Geographic Survey of the Territories, conducted geological mapping and natural history surveys of Colorado in the summers of 1873 through 1876, during which his parties visited most of the high country. The results were reported in a series of annual descriptive reports and produced the *Geological and Geographical Atlas of Colorado* (1877), a pioneering topographical work. Major John Wesley Powell (1834–1902), who gained national attention in 1869 by successfully leading an exploring party some nine hundred miles down the Green and Colorado rivers and through the Grand Canyon, conducted the government surveys in Colorado and Utah, beginning in 1871. Clarence King (1842–1901), after serving as an assistant in the California State Geological Survey (1863–66), was placed in charge of the Fortieth Parallel Survey, which scientifically explored a hundred-mile strip from eastern Colorado to the border of California (1867–72). The work of all three was in no small measure responsible for creating an image of the American West as an exciting and attractive place to visit.

Powell, Hayden, and King are all connected with the mountaineering history of Estes Park. Powell, together with William N. Byers, the founding editor of the *Rocky Mountain News,* and five others, made the first ascent of Longs Peak on August 23, 1868. Hayden conducted the first woman, the well-known author and lecturer Anna E. Dickinson, to the top of Longs Peak on September 13, 1873. Two years earlier, in August 1871, King climbed Longs Peak in the company of Bostonian Henry Adams, who had come to Estes Park as a tourist. All three parties were taken by the beauty of the place. "Not only has nature supplied this valley with features of rare beauty and surroundings of admirable grandeur," noted the Hayden Survey Report for 1875, "but it has thus distributed them that the eye of an artist may rest with perfect satisfaction on the complete picture presented." *Ninth Annual Report of the United States Geological and Geographical Survey of the Territories ... By F. V. Hayden* (Washington: Government Printing Office, 1877), p. 437.

10:12. Horace Ferguson (1826–1912) was not drawn to Colorado from Missouri by gold (as "a pioneer of '59") but rather because of his wife's bronchial asthma, and then not until 1870. He first came to Estes Park in the fall of 1874 to hunt, fish, "and take a look around." Ferguson decided to stay, homesteading half a mile north of Marys Lake, which was then, as Chapin notes, "a small sheet of alkaline water ... formerly a great resort for big-horn, elk, and deer, which came in great numbers to the lake, as they would to a salt-lick." By April 1875, Ferguson had completed a two-room cabin and moved his family from their home near Greeley and was soon guiding trout fishermen into Moraine Park to fish the Big Thompson (See, for example, Charles F. Orvis and A. Nelson Cheney, eds., *Fishing with the Fly: Sketches by Lovers of the Art* [Manchester, Vt.: C. F. Orvis, 1883], pp. 131–41). Homestead slowly evolved into resort. Four rooms were added to the cabin in 1877. "This was the beginning of our boarding career," Horace Ferguson's youngest daughter, Sally, recalled years later, "although the summer before one eastern lady stayed with us sleeping in a tent and having her meals in the kitchen with the family." Enlarged again in 1878 with the addition of a kitchen and dining room, "the Highlands," as the Fergusons would rename their ranch, could eventually accommodate some twenty-five paying guests in its main building, five three-room cottages, and five tent houses. Horace Ferguson was widely known for his prowess as a hunter. On one occasion he shot a brown bear on the shores of Bear Lake, thus giving the lake its name.

11:23. The *Appalachia* articles were published as follows: "The First Ascent of a Glacier in Colorado," 5 (December 1887): 1–12; "The Ascent of Long's Peak," 5 (June 1888): 109–21; "Ypsilon Peak," 5 (December 1888): 175–83. Chapin's brief February 1889 *Scribner's Magazine* article (5: 215–18) was entitled "Photographing the Big-Horn."

12:10. John Merle Coulter, *Manual of the Botany of the Rocky*

Mountain Region (New York: Ivison, Blakeman, Taylor, and Company, 1885). Coulter (1851–1928) began to collect plants in 1872 while serving as assistant geologist on the Hayden Survey. Hayden named him botanist and assigned him to the Photographic Division of the 1873 Survey led by William H. Jackson. Their party spent three days in Estes Park, May 29–June 1, 1873.

12:12. Mr. and Mrs. George Thacher of Boston were guests at the Highlands during Chapin's 1887 and 1888 visits. On May 6, 1889, Mrs. Thacher read a paper entitled "Alpine Flowers of Colorado" before a meeting of the Appalachian Mountain Club. This paper, which includes details of her stay in Estes Park and her climb to the Keyhole on Longs Peak in the company of Carlyle Lamb, was published in the May 1889 issue of *Appalachia* (5: 284–91).

CHAPTER I: "ESTES PARK"

13:6. Fremont's Peak is located in west-central Wyoming.

13:16. The barometric readings of mountain elevations given by Chapin have since been revised by the U.S. Geological Survey.

14:16. Chapin made an unsuccessful attempt to climb this mountain in July 1887. See Foreword, n. 33.

15:26. The allusion is to Windham Thomas Wyndham-Quin (1841–1926), the fourth Earl of Dunraven, whose attempt to gain control of Estes Park is discussed above. In 1907, Freelan O. Stanley of Boston, the inventor of the Stanley Steamer, and his partner Burton D. Sanborn, a Greeley developer, finally succeeded in purchasing the earl's residual interests of some 6,600 acres. Dunraven wrote an article about his first (1872) visit to Estes Park, entitled "A Colorado Sketch," for the September 1880 issue of *Nineteenth Century* (8: 445–57) and briefly recalled his Estes Park experiences in his two-volume autobiography, *Past Times and Pastimes* 1 (London: Hodder and Stoughton, 1922), 140–43.

16:1. In 1876 Dunraven decided to build a cottage for himself and a hotel for his friends. That year the noted landscape artist Albert Bierstadt (1830–1902), whom Dunraven had invited to Colorado on commission to paint Longs Peak, helped pick out the sites on Fish Creek Road because of their magnificent view. The three-story, fifty-room English (or Estes Park) Hotel, with its wrap-around porches and artificial lake in front, opened in July 1877. S. Anna Gordon, who visited the hotel shortly afterward, noted that "The building is richly furnished, and is conducted in a manner to please the most fastidious patrons." (*Camping in Colorado* [New York: W. B. Smith & Co., 1882], p. 109.) Following Dunraven's departure, the English Hotel, the first tourist hotel in Colorado, passed into other hands and burned in August 1911. His cottage, however, still survives. Dunraven also built a hunting lodge sequestered on the North Fork of the Big Thompson River in a small park known as Dunraven Glade, where he brought hunting parties into the late 1880s. The story of the Bierstadt-Dunraven relationship is told in Gordon Hendrick, *Albert Bierstadt: Painter of the American West* (New York: Harry N. Abrams, 1974), pp. 250–53. The chief legacy of Bierstadt's Estes Park visit is the magnificent five-foot by eight-foot painting, *Rocky Mountains, Longs Peak,* which now hangs in the Western Room of the Denver Public Library.

16:3. In addition to Ferguson's, the other four ranches taking in summer guests undoubtedly were those of Abner Sprague (1850–1943), who homesteaded in Moraine Park (or Willow Park as it was then called) in 1875; Alexander Q. MacGregor (1845–96), who homesteaded the mouth of the Black Canyon in 1875, and offered cabin accommodations and encouraged tenting on the hillside north of Black Canyon Creek; William E. James (?–1895), who established Elkhorn Lodge on Fall River west of Dunraven's property in 1877; and the Reverend Elkanah Lamb (1832–1915), whose ranch, Longs Peak House in the Tahosa Valley, Chapin discusses below. Sprague's ranch ultimately was sold in 1904 and operated as Stead's Ranch and Hotel until its buildings and 560 acres of land were purchased by the National Park Service in 1962 and razed. The James's lodge, which still stands, gave its name to Elkhorn Avenue, the main thoroughfare of the village of Estes Park.

16:12. Muggins Gulch begins southeast of the summit of Park Hill along the road to Lyons (Route 36). According to Milton Estes (1840–1913), the son of pioneer Joel Estes, "Muggins Gulch was named for George Hearst, whose nickname was 'Muggins.' He was given this name by Dan Grant, who with a man called

Sowers had some cattle in the Park, and 'Muggins' was their her-
der. Muggins built a cabin at the head of the gulch so he could
watch the cattle, lest any should try to leave and go back to the
valley." (Milton Estes, "Memoirs of Estes Park," *Colorado Magazine* 16 [July 1939]: 127.) Muggins Gulch subsequently became
the site of the crude log cabin of James Nugent, "Rocky Mountain
Jim," who came to Estes Park in 1868 and five years later, in
October 1873, conducted the indomitable Englishwoman
Isabella Bird (1831–1904) to the top of Longs Peak. She recorded
her adventure in *A Lady's Life in the Rocky Mountains* (London:
John Murray, 1879).

16:20. The Reverend Elkanah J. Lamb (1832–1915), an
itinerant preacher, was Longs Peak's first professional guide. His
160-acre homestead on the eastern slope of Longs Peak became
the site of Longs Peak House, from where the Reverend Lamb
and his son Carlyle guided parties of visitors to the top of the
peak. Chapin's facts about Lamb's life are not wholly correct.
Born in Indiana, Lamb did briefly prospect for gold in the Tar-
ryall district in South Park in 1860, but lived in Kansas and Nebraska before returning to Colorado in the spring of 1871 as a
minister of the Church of the United Brethren in the St. Vrain
valley. That August he visited Estes Park and made his first ascent of Longs Peak. Following a two-year appointment in the
western parts of Nebraska and Kansas, Lamb returned once
more to Colorado in the fall of 1873. Two years later, in 1875,
Lamb constructed the twelve-by-fourteen-foot cabin covered by
poles, brush, and dirt in the Tahosa Valley that would evolve into
Longs Peak House. Soon afterward Lamb was augmenting his
preacher's salary by raising cattle, putting up tourists, and guiding parties to the summit for five dollars a trip. "If they would not
pay for spiritual guidance," Lamb later wrote, "I compelled them
to divide for material elevation." Lamb continued to operate
Longs Peak House until 1902, when he sold it to Enos Mills
(1870–1922), the celebrated naturalist and guide who was in
good measure responsible for the creation of Rocky Mountain
National Park in 1915. After Longs Peak House was destroyed by
fire in 1906, Mills rebuilt Longs Peak Inn to his own distinctive
specifications and continued to operate it until the time of his
death in 1922. Lamb left a record of his Estes Park experiences in

two autobiographical volumes, *Memories of the Past and Thoughts of the Future* (United Brethren Publishing House, 1906) and *Miscellaneous Meditations* (Publishers' Press Room and Bindery Company, [c. 1913?]).

18:16. As Chapin himself notes in Chapter II, Lily Mountain is actually the Twin Sisters. F. V. Hayden's atlases of 1877 and 1881 label the Twin Sisters as Lillie Mountain. The confusion between the Twin Sisters and its near neighbor, now known as Lily Mountain (9,786 feet), continued into the early twentieth century. In 1887–88 present-day Lily Mountain was still unnamed.

18:24. Sheep Mountain was an early name for Rams Horn Mountain.

19:12. At 11,225 feet, Mount Hood in Oregon's Cascade Mountains is the highest point in the state.

19:n. Andrew Wilson, *Abode of Snow: Observations on a Journey from Chinese Tibet to the Indian Caucasus* (New York: G. P. Putnam's Sons, 1875).

21:6. Now called the Never Summer Range.

22:1. See **16:3** above.

23:11. See **16:1** above.

CHAPTER 2: "LONG'S PEAK"

23:9. Sharp, crested ridges.

25:16. Now called Flattop Mountain. The mountain was apparently unnamed until Chapin and William L. Hallett's 1887 climb.

27:27. This wagon road, which followed an older hunting trail into Estes Park and generally follows present Route 7, was cut in the fall of 1875 and the spring of 1876 by Elkanah and Carlyle Lamb to allow access to their Longs Peak House. During its first years the Lambs operated it as a toll road. The route is clearly visible in Hayden's 1877 atlas.

29:4. Now the Tahosa Valley, but then known as Longs Peak Valley.

29:27. Carlyle Lamb (1862–1958), ten years Chapin's junior, first ascended Longs Peak with his father, mother, and brother in 1879. He became a guide in 1880 and for the next twenty-two years made some 146 trips to the summit. It was Carlyle Lamb, rather than his father, who in 1889 secured formal title to the 160-acre tract at the base of Longs Peak on which Longs Peak House stood. In 1902 he sold the property to Enos Mills.

30:24. Sylvester Dunham, "An Ascent of Long's Peak," *Good Company* 7 (March–April 1881): 31–37.

32:19. Alpine Creek.

32:24. This trail was built by Abner Sprague's brother, Fred (1857–1922), who also had a homestead in Willow (Moraine) Park. It approached the Boulderfield from the north along the west branch of Wind River, climbed the west side of Battle Mountain, and then joined the trail from Longs Peak House at Granite Pass.

36:22. Carrie J. Welton, a wealthy and eccentric native of Waterbury, Connecticut, became the first woman to die on Longs Peak on September 23, 1884. Her guide was Carlyle Lamb. When she and Lamb reached the Keyhole the wind was blowing hard and clouds were gathering, but she refused to turn back. They reached the summit successfully, but Miss Welton was exhausted. Lamb helped her down as far as the Keyhole. It was then midnight and Lamb was forced to go for help. It was five miles to the Lamb cabin, and by the time that Carlyle returned with his father Carrie Welton was dead. Elkanah Lamb discusses the incident in some detail in his *Miscellaneous Meditations* (pp. 78–88).

40:1. The minutes of the February 9, 1887, meeting of the Appalachian Mountain Club notes: "A letter from Mr. F. H. Chapin, describing his ascent of Pike's Peak, was read by Mr. F. W. Freeborn." *Appalachia* 5 (1887–89): 83. The climb took place in the summer of 1886.

41:9. The Grand River was officially renamed the Colorado River in 1921.

41:15. Grays Peak (14,270 feet) and Torreys Peak (14,267 feet), named in 1861 after famous botanists Asa Gray and John Torrey, are located in the Front Range near Georgetown and were frequently climbed during Chapin's day. The Mount of the Holy Cross (14,005 feet), to the west, in whose crevices the snow never melts, gained national attention through the photographs taken in 1873 by William H. Jackson and through Henry Wadsworth Longfellow's famous sonnet of 1879.

41:22. Chapin is incorrect. A number of other nearby mountains exceed Mummy Mountain's 13,425 feet. These include Chiefs Head (13,579), Mount Ypsilon (13,514), Fairchild Mountain (13,502), Hagues Peak (13,506), Mount Meeker (13,911), and Pagoda Mountain (13,497).

41:26. Now known as Forest Canyon.

43:n. *Report of the Geological Exploration of the Fortieth Parallel,* vol. 2, *Descriptive Geology, by Arnold Hague and S. F. Emmons* (Washington: Government Printing Office, 1877).

44:4. Edward Whymper, *The Ascent of the Matterhorn* (London: John Murray, 1880), p. 227.

44:12. Chapin himself had looked out upon the Matterhorn from Zermatt during his summer 1877 visit. Chapin did not climb the Matterhorn, though his traveling companion, Charles P. Howard of Hartford, did. Chapin climbed the Zinal Rothhorn during his second visit to Switzerland in June 1882.

45:1. The Bunker Hill monument, completed in 1842, is a 221-foot granite obelisk that stands on Breed's Hill across the Charles River from Boston.

46:16. Chasm Lake (11,760 feet), which lies in a glacial cirque beneath the sheer east face of Longs Peak.

49:7. Chapin and his companions were looking down upon some of the many lakes in Wild Basin, an area largely ignored by early visitors.

51:1. Mills Glacier, like Mills Moraine, which Chapin calls attention to below, was later named for Enos Mills (1870–1922), who from 1902 until the time of his death owned and operated his famous inn at the foot of Longs Peak.

52:13. Benjamin Ives Gilman (1852–1933), an ethnomusicologist who pioneered the study of music of the Zuni and Hopi Indians, served for many years as secretary of the Boston Museum of Fine Arts. In 1888, Gilman had recently completed several years of graduate study in Germany and France.

57:10. The south lateral moraine in Willow (Moraine) Park provides one of the best examples of the region's glacial history.

58:12. Compact granular snow that forms on a glacier.

58:12. Gullies or ravines.

61:15. Probably Tahosa Creek, which meanders along the floor of Tahosa Valley and enters the North Fork of the St. Vrain River.

64:1. William L. Hallett (1851–1941), a native of Springfield, Massachusetts, and an engineering graduate of MIT, first came to Estes Park with his mother during the summer of 1878, and briefly stayed at the one-year-old English Hotel on Fish Creek Road before moving to Horace Ferguson's Highlands. The following winter Hallett married and returned to Estes Park with his bride for a thirty-day camping trip to Grand Lake and back, guided by Abner Sprague. In 1881, having decided to exchange engineering for ranching, the Halletts erected a summer home, Edgemont, on three acres of land provided by Horace Ferguson near the Highlands. For the next several summers, when he was not taking care of the cattle that he drove up into the park from their winter home west of Loveland, William Hallett explored the region in the company of mountain adventurers like Frederick Chapin. The Hallett house still stands to the north of Marys Lake.

68:19. This expedition would have taken Chapin and his party up Forest Canyon (or Willow Canyon, as it was then called).

CHAPTER 3: "MOUNT HALLETT"

69:5. Hagues Peak is named for Lieutenant Arnold Hague (1840–1917), a geologist who, as a member of Clarence King's Geological Survey of the Fortieth Parallel, used the mountain as a triangulation point. Hague accompanied Clarence King and Henry Adams to the top of Longs Peak in 1871. Hagues Peak is one of the few landmarks in the Estes Park area labeled in the King atlas of 1876; it is also identified in the Hayden atlas of 1877.

70:9. A surveyor's instrument for measuring horizontal and vertical angles.

71:25. William L. Hallett. See Chapter 2, 64:1.

72:3. Hallett peak (12,713 feet), in 1887 not yet named.

72:5. Tyndall Glacier, which is in fact "a true glacier," is named for the noted British scientist and mountaineer John Tyndall (1820–93), who was especially interested in glaciation. The name was apparently first suggested by Enos Mills, though it was not officially adopted by the National Park Service until 1932.

72:13. As Chapin himself indicates in a footnote in Chapter V, "the surgeon" was Dr. Edward Osgood Otis (1848–1933) of Boston. Born in Rye, New Hampshire, Otis received his undergraduate and medical degrees from Harvard, and then established a practice in Boston as a specialist in pulmonary diseases, particularly tuberculosis. One of Otis's interests was climatology and he authored a number of papers on health resorts. Like Charles E. Fay, mentioned below, Otis was for many years on the faculty of Tufts College. At the time of his visit to Colorado he was a member of the surgical staff of the Boston Dispensary. Otis Peak (12,486 feet), just south of Hallet Peak, is named in his honor. Otis apparently enjoyed his Colorado experience, for he soon became an official member of the Appalachian Mountain Club. Chapin's other companion, the "member of the Appalachian Mountain Club," was undoubtedly George W. Thacher of Boston. See Preface, n. 12:12.

72:14. Until 1914, the only trail up Flattop (Table) mountain was by way of Mill Creek Basin. In the winter of 1876–77, Horace Ferguson and Abner Sprague established a camp to cut shingles for cottages on Steep Mountain above Mill Creek and built a wagon road to it. A year later, during the fall and winter of 1877–78, two men named Hill and Beckwith established a sawmill near where the overflow from Bierstadt Lake above runs into Mill Creek, thus giving the creek its name (see Chapin's reference below). Loggers and woodsmen were brought in from Wisconsin to do the work, and until the fall of 1880, when Hill and Beckwith moved the mill to the booming mining town of Teller in North Park, their Estes Park operation was a busy one. A few logs and a foundation are all that remain of the site.

73:13. Mill Creek.

73:24. Undoubtedly, Alice Chapin and Mrs. George Thacher.

74:10. The trail up Flattop Mountain provides dramatic overlook views of both Dream and Emerald lakes.

74:23. The lake nestling into Glacier Gorge to the southeast is undoubtedly Mills Lake, named by Abner Sprague after Enos Mills.

76:18. The Berkshire Mountains of western Massachusetts.

81:8. See Chapter 6, 120:7.

81:18. A small, extremely shy, goat-like antelope that is native to the high mountain regions of Europe and the Caucases. Chamois are difficult to hunt, or capture in photographs, because of their alertness and quickness.

82:2. The passage quoted occurs near the end of chapter fifteen of John Tyndall's *The Glaciers of the Alps, Being a Narrative of Excursions and Ascents, An Account of the Origin and Phenomena of Glaciers, And an Exposition of the Physical Principles to Which They Are Related* (London: John Murray, 1860).

82:21. William A. Baillie-Grohman, *Camps in the Rockies. Being A Narrative of Life on the Frontier, and Sport in the Rocky Mountains, With an Account of the Cattle Ranches of the West* (London: Sampson Low, Marston, Searle, & Rivington, 1883).

82:23. William S. Rainsford, "Camping and Hunting in the Shoshone," *Scribner's Magazine* 1 (September 1887): 292–311.

82:n. John James Audubon, *The Quadrupeds of North America, by John J. Audubon . . . and the Rev. John Bachman* (New York: V. G. Audubon, 1851–54.)

84:25. Chapin's reference is to the Topographical Party of the Hayden Survey, which carried out measurements in the Estes Park area in 1873 under the direction of Hayden's principal assistant, James T. Gardiner (1842–1912).

86:12. Glacial fissure.

CHAPTER 4: "TABLE MOUNTAIN"

88:1. Western slang for personal gear or effects.

94:4. John Rayner Edmands (1850–1910) was born in Boston and educated as an engineer at MIT, where he received his degree in 1869. Edmands served for many years as an assistant for the Harvard College Observatory and during the summer of 1887 was a member of the party under Observatory director Edward C. Pickering, which mounted a twelve-inch telescope on the summit of Pikes Peak. Edmands' chief avocational interest was the Appalachian Mountain Club, in whose activities he played an extremely active role for many years.

94:4. Charles Ernest Fay (1846–1931) was born in Roxbury, Massachusetts, and educated at Tufts College, where he received both B.A. and M.A. degrees. In 1871, following a year of travel abroad, Fay returned to Tufts as Wade professor of modern languages, a position he would occupy for some fifty-seven years. A founding member of the Appalachian Mountain Club in 1876 and the American Alpine Club in 1902, Fay won international attention for his achievements in exploration and mountaineering. He climbed extensively in New Hampshire's White Mountains and, later, in the Canadian Rockies (his name adorns 10,612-foot Mt. Fay, in the Lake Louise district). In July 1926, Fay and his wife briefly returned to Estes Park and at the suggestion of Roger Toll, superintendent of the Rocky Mountain National Park, wrote a brief article recalling his earlier visit of 1888 ("Professor Fay Recounts Visit in Rocky Mountains in 1888," *Estes Park Trail* 6 [July 23, 1926]: 3, 18). The Fay Lakes below Mount Ypsilon have been named to commemorate his mountaineering expeditions with Frederick Chapin.

96:18. John Burroughs (1837–1921), the philosopher-naturalist. The quotation is from *Locusts and Wild Honey,* a volume of nature essays (Boston: Houghton Osgood and Company, 1879).

CHAPTER 5: "MUMMY MOUNTAIN"

97:13. The peaks of the Mummy Range include Mount Chapin, Mount Chiquita, Mount Ypsilon, Fairchild Mountain, Mummy Mountain, and Hagues Peak.

97:15. Chapin may be confused. Hallett (Rowe) Glacier, a large crescent of ice partly surrounding a small tarn, sits below Hagues Peak, not Mummy Mountain.

97:16. The "recent developments" is a reference to the article in the September 1887 issue of *Science* by George H. Stone (1841–1917), a professor of geology at Colorado College, reporting the discovery of Hallett Glacier and the visit made two months earlier by Chapin and his companions. "A Living Glacier on Hague's Peak, Colorado," *Science* 10 (September 23, 1887): 153–54. Less than three weeks later, on October 12, 1887, Chapin presented his own account of his trip to the glacier, "The First Ascent of a Glacier in Colorado," to the members of the Appalachian Mountain Club. See Chapter 8, **147:14.**

97:17. Israel Rowe (?–1884) first came to Estes Park in 1875 to work as assistant foreman on the toll road into the park being constructed by Alexander MacGregor (see Chapter 1, **16:3**) and built a cabin at the foot of Mount Olympus. Following the road's completion, Rowe decided to remain and for a number of years supported himself and his family by means of his prowess as a hunter and a guide. He discovered the glacier that Chapin calls

"Hallett" while guiding a party of guests from Dunraven's English Hotel. Rowe left Estes Park in 1882 and died soon afterward while on a hunting trip in Wyoming. In 1932, at the recommendation of the National Park Service, the glacier below Hagues Peak was renamed "Rowe Glacier" in honor of its discoverer.

98:15. Hallett's near-fatal fall into a glacial fissure, which occured in 1883, is recounted by Chapin below. Like Tyndall Glacier, Hallett (Rowe) Glacier is one of the five living or "true" glaciers within the boundaries of Rocky Mountain National Park.

99:7. Chapin identifies this other "member of the Appalachian Mountain Club" as George W. Thacher of Boston in the presentation that he delivered to the AMC in October 1887. See Preface, **12:12**.

99:13. The Black Canyon is so-called because of what one 1878 visitor described as "its thick growth of pines and black and gloomy shadows." Carrie Adell Strahorn, *Fifteen Thousand Miles by Stage* (New York: G. P. Putnam's Sons, 1911), pp. 68–69.

104:10. Humboldt Glacier in northwest Greenland is the world's largest known glacier.

114:7. The reference is unclear; there are some seventeen Bald Mountains in Colorado, a number of them in or near the Front Range.

115:9. Vacuum.

116:n. Joseph LeConte, "On Some of the Ancient Glaciers of the Sierras," *American Journal of Sciences and Arts* 5 (May 1873): 332–33.

CHAPTER 6: "YPSILON PEAK"

120:7. According to Joel Estes, Jr., when his father first entered Estes Park in October 1859, the only visible signs of Indians were old poles that looked as if they had been whacked with a tomahawk. Abner Sprague, who homesteaded in Moraine Park in 1875, reported that lodge poles were still standing in several places. Nevertheless, given the passage of time and the influx of visitors, it seems likely that the pile of poles that Chapin encountered, however romantic they may have appeared, were the work of other, more recent, hands.

124:27. In 1888 the wagon road into Horseshoe Park extended as far as Roaring River, then yet unnamed.

130:6. These two lakes at the base of Mount Ypsilon were subsequently named the Spectacle Lakes by Roger Toll in 1922. Toll, superintendent of Rocky Mountain National Park, thought the two lakes resembled a pair of eyeglasses.

131:22. Lulu City was a short-lived mining camp in Middle Park just across the Continental Divide from Estes Park, which in its boom years of 1880–83 boasted plans for a 160-acre town and 3,000–5,000 citizens. A well-known photograph of July 28, 1889, taken less than ten years later, shows the town abandoned and in an advanced state of decay. Michigan City was an equally short-lived mining camp situated north of Lulu City near the summit of Cameron Pass, an important entrance to North Park. Named after the Michigan Mine, the camp's life paralleled Lulu City's. Both Lulu City and Michigan City are clearly labeled on *Nell's Topographical & Township Map of the State of Colorado* (Washington, 1885).

132:27. A saddle or depression between two mountains.

CHAPTER 7: "HAGUE'S PEAK"

137:4. This outcropping along Lumpy Ridge, slightly to the northeast of the village of Estes Park, has long since been called (perhaps because of Chapin's comparison) the Twin Owls.

141:7. These are Crystal Lake and Little Crystal Lake, which lie above Lawn Lake on the northeastern slope of Fairchild Mountain.

141:8. This "notch" between Fairchild and Hagues Peak is now known as The Saddle.

CHAPTER 8: "STONE'S PEAK"

147:14. Stones Peak, named after Profesor George H. Stone of Colorado College. See Chapter 5, **97:16.**

149:3. This unnamed creek is undoubtedly Hidden River, which flows out of Spruce Canyon.

154:1. Hayden Spire, so-named by Abner Sprague in 1911 after Julian Hayden (1886–1964) who together with his brother Al explored the Estes Park area during the first years of the twentieth century.

155:15. Though once believed to have been an extinct volcano, geologists have now established that Specimen Mountain

(12,489 feet) and the adjacent Crater to the southwest are formed of ash and other volcanic material from an eruption that took place elsewhere. Early tourists noted the sheep trails leading over into The Crater and the area still remains a good place to watch for the elusive bighorn.

155:23. Sprague Glacier, one of the five true glaciers in what is now Rocky Mountain National Park. Like nearby Sprague Mountain and Sprague Pass, as well as Sprague Lake, it is named for Estes Park pioneer Abner E. Sprague (1850–1943). Sprague Glacier was named by Enos Mills in 1905.

156:3. Chapin is referring to one of the three lakes at the base of Sprague Glacier, known collectively until 1961 as the Rainbow Lakes. The largest is now called Rainbow Lake, the smallest Lake Irene, and the third has no name at all.

159:4. Forest Canyon.